■ TABLE OF CONTENTS

Introduction - 5
Kit Grades - 7
Instruction Symbol Guide - 8

History of Gunpla - 11
Pre Gundam - 11
Freedom Fighter - 12
Bronson Connection & Original Reception - 14
Origin of Gunpla - 15
The Gunpla Boom - 16
Gunpla Backlash & Plamo Kyoshiro - 17
MSV Line & Zeta Gundam - 19
End of the Boom - 21
World Resurgence - 22

Tools - 23
Knives - 25
Side Cutters & Cutting Mats - 26
Files, Sandpaper & Tweezers - 27
Skewers & Putty - 28
Sticky Tack & Glue/Cement - 29
Markers - 32

Paint & Thinner Basics - 33
Water Based Paints - 35
Oil Based Paints - 36
Paint Type Comparison - 37
Topcoat Finishes - 41

1/144 HG Exia Gundam - 43
How to Find Parts
& Cutting Parts from the Sprue - 44
Prebuilding Techniques - 45
Cleaning Parts - 46
Cementing & Sanding - 48
Seamline Removal - 49
Panel Lining - 50
Top Coat Application - 51

1/100 NG Blaze Zaku Phantom - 55
Model Kit Planning, Sanding & Mistakes - 56
Gap & Seamline Removal - 57
Masking & Painting - 58
Chipping & Weathering - 61

1/144 HGUC RX-78-2 Gundam - 67
Articulation Modding - 68
Subtractive Mods - 69
Puttying your Kit - 71
Primer Preparations - 72
Spray Can Anatomy - 73
Priming - 74
Simulated Paint Chips - 75
Sticker & Decal Application - 76

1/100 HG Deathscythe Hell Custom - 79
Model Kit Planning - 80
Filing Seams & Sink Marks - 81
Deepening Panel Lines & Sanding Seamlines After Masking - 82
Mistakes After Priming & Spraying Mistakes - 83
Masking - 84
Enamel Panel Line Wash - 86
Shading with Gundam Markers - 87

In Conclusion - 91

コレクション No. 36
マゼラ・アタック
MAGELLA·ATTACK
0008676 400 **BANDAI** BANDAI PLASTIC MODEL KIT MADE IN JAPAN
カラー塗装説明図付

1:1200 SCALE 機動戦士 **ガンダム**
ジオン軍巡弾艦
ベストメカ コレクション No. 5 量産型 **ムサイ**
0008666 300 **BANDAI** BANDAI PLASTIC MODEL KIT MADE IN JAPAN
カラー塗装説明図付

WEAPONS FOR MOBILE SUIT 機動戦士 **ガンダム**
1:144 SCALE
モビルスーツ用
ベストメカ コレクション No. 16 武器セット
0008664 300 **BANDAI** BANDAI PLASTIC MODEL KIT MADE IN JAPAN
カラー塗装説明図付

M.S NORMAL TYPE
1:144 SCALE ジオン軍モビルスーツ 機動戦士 **ガンダム**
水陸両用 タイプ **アッガイ**
ベストメカ コレクション No. 22 MSM-04
0008661 **BANDAI** BANDAI PLASTIC MODEL KIT MADE IN JAPAN
カラー塗装説明図付

1:1200 SCALE 機動戦士 **ガンダム**
ジオン軍巡弾艦
ベストメカ コレクション No. 13 シャア専用 **ムサイ**
0008665 **BANDAI** BANDAI PLASTIC MODEL KIT MADE IN JAPAN
カラー塗装説明図付

1:2400 SCALE 機動戦士 **ガンダム**
ジオン軍大型戦闘艦
ベストメカ コレクション No. 53 **グワジン**
0008745 300 **BANDAI** BANDAI PLASTIC MODEL KIT MADE IN JAPAN
カラー塗装説明図付

1:1200 SCALE 機動戦士 **ガンダム**
ジオン軍巡弾艦
ベストメカ コレクション No. 13 シャア専用 **ムサイ**
0008665 300 **BANDAI** カラー塗装説明図付

WEAPONS FOR MOBILE SUIT 機動戦士 **ガンダム**
1:144

左側の箱（上から下へ）:
カラー塗装説明図付
塗装説明図付
ー塗装説明図付
カラー塗装説明図付
カラー塗装説明図付

右側の箱（上から下へ）:
N
006
M.S N Z 1:144 SCALE ベストメカ コレクシ **No. 4** 0008675
M.S N 1:144 SCALE ベストメ コレクショ **No. 6** 0008652
1:1200 ジ ベストメカ コレクション **No. 13** 0008665

1:144 コア 大気
ベストメカ コレクション No. 43 0008674

1:1200

■ INTRODUCTION
x Stan Hyde

Let's start with the bottom line: *you build models of things that you love.*

Model building, even if you're doing a good job, takes too much time otherwise. What keeps you going through all the problem-solving, mistakes, and wrong paths (that lead into new discoveries) is the fact that, eventually, you are going to wind up with a scale representation of something you REALLY like! It doesn't matter whether it's hot cars or science fiction spacecraft, military dioramas or submarines. You build those subjects because you care.

The history of plastic models is too big to cover here, but the plastic model hobby really took off after World War Two.

Among other things, there were a lot of builders who were interested in building scale replicas of real things . . . often real things that

had been shooting at them, and especially the real things that help shoot back. Planes, tanks, and military vehicles were, at one time and still to a large degree are, the backbone of the modeling hobby.

Now, fast-forward a decade or so later, and a new generation appears. Though this is a generalization, they were interested in two things. First, when they were younger: monsters. Then, when they were old enough to date: cars.

My generation is called the "Monster Kid" generation, which stretched from the late 50's into the 70's and includes people like George Lucas and Stephen Spielberg and, later, Peter Jackson. We grew up reading about special effects and monster movies, and we knew that models were used to make the special effects in a lot of those movies. We really liked monsters!

So it's no surprise that, in 1961 when Aurora models brought out the first movie monster model (Frankenstein from the 1931 movie), we were there. Followed quickly by Dracula, the Mummy, the Wolfman, and later King Kong and Godzilla ... my generation grew up building monsters.

There were even monster hot rods, like Frankenstein's Flivver, which combined the hot rod car genre with the monster genre.

Now, unlike the previous generation, starting in the 1960's model kits were no longer necessarily scale representations of "real things." You could argue that the monsters - from King Kong to the Creature of the Black Lagoon - were "real." Stop-motion models and costumes were used to bring those creatures to life on the screen, so it could be argued you were building a model of a costume or, well, a model of a model.

But most of us really felt we were building King Kong, or whichever monster was our favorite at the time.

Models had taken a big leap. They were no longer just scale replicas of 'real things,' they were now interpretations of film and science fiction subjects.

They were, perhaps, moving toward art. What mattered wasn't just the accuracy of the kit, but the kit sculptor's interpretation of the subject. How it looked became very important.

Flash-forward to 1979, and a new anime series debuts on Japanese television, GUNDAM. It wasn't the first robot show, or the first show to have plastic models fashioned after the robots, but it did deal with the subject of giant, pilot-driven humanoid machines (really, mecha; not robots) in a way that blended social commentary, science fiction, war stories, and even realism to create something that was unique. A new generation of fans grew up loving it!

Can you see a pattern developing here ... ?

Starting in 1980, the first Gundam models, Gunpla - Gundam plastic model kits - appeared. Fans and Bandai, the company most associated with Gunpla, have never looked back.

If you're reading this book, you probably love building Mecha. In the model world, these machines represent a unique blend of figure building and vehicle building. Like figures, they are posable and their poses represent a story - or at least an incident - which is being depicted by the model kit. At the same time, many of the skills needed to build these kits come from the skills required for building vehicles. Though they are science fiction subjects, the models themselves exist in the real world, so custom paint jobs, damage from use, and even rust can be an appropriate part of your interpretation of them as a subject.

In other words, when you build Mecha you have to use two sets of eyes: your model builder's "accurate representation of the real world" eyes, and your artist's "how can I tell the story most dramatically" eyes.

So, with all this to be concerned about, where do you start? Well, you've chosen the right place. This book is an introduction to what you really need to know to get started building Mecha.

Often, I am complemented for my model building skills and feel a little badly about it, because so much of being successful with models is knowing the time-saving tricks and methods that bring a three dimensional object to life. But that's true of all craftsmen and artists. A large part of the work is knowing the basics.

And that's what you have here: all the information you need to get started. If you can save time on the fundamentals, then you can lavish all that extra time - that 'love' time - on making things look really good.

So read this book carefully and practice the skills that are presented here until they're part of what you bring to a new model every time you open the box.

There's really nothing like opening that box and seeing those pieces, and having the confidence to know that you are going to create something that will stand out.

Artist or crafts-person, whichever you like to call yourself, you're on a path of discovery, because it's your own individual observations of the real world and your own individual ideas about what is dramatic that will eventually make your model kits unlike anybody else's.

Ultimately, spending time to learn these skills is all about expressing yourself in solid, visible, three-dimensional terms. It's about showing yourself, your friends, and the world what you really like.

So get reading, get building, and show us what you love!

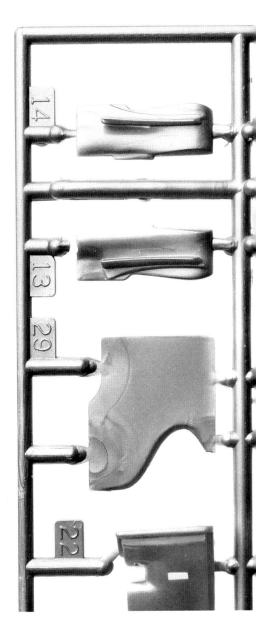

■ KIT GRADES

No Grade kits exist in 1/60, 1/100, and 1/144 scales and, depending on the scale and the era they were created in, differ greatly in quality and engineering. No Grade kits are often a cheaper alternative to their MG or HG counterparts. They can also be designs that weren't popular enough to get a MG or HG release, or could simply be a kit created before 2000.

Introduced in the early 1990's, High Grade kits feature improved articulation, color separation and polycap joints. They are a budget alternative to the more costly Master Grades. The HGUC (High Grade Universal Century) line is wildly popular, and has well over 150 kits currently available. Most HG kits are 1/144 scale.

Beginning in 1995, these kits were designed to place emphasis on internal details, such as actuators, pistons, and detailed thrusters. MGs often include decals that are either "dry rub" (the majority) or "water slide" for more details. Only the most popular mobile suit designs are released as MG kits.

PERFECT GRADE

Perfect Grade kits are 1/60 scale, and are among the largest, most detailed kits available. Due to the incredible cost for these kits, only the most popular designs are ever released. Costing well into the hundreds of dollars, Perfect Grades feature LED gimmicks, metal parts and hudreds of plastic parts.

Real Grade is one of the newest lines, with only a few kits released at the time of this writing. The Real Grade line is an attempt to bring the detail and proportions of the Master Grade line, into a more economically priced 1/144 scale. While more expensive than the majority of HG kits, the Real Grades have proven to be popular, with the best articulation currently available.

The Mega Size model line was released to coincide with the 30th anniversary of Mobile Suit Gundam. Towering at a massive 1/48 scale, these kits are among the biggest ever commercially released, and are essentially a scaled up version of their HG counterparts. The kits feature very few parts, and very little detail, but offer a great value for less than the cost of some Master Grades.

Super Deformed kits, known as Superior Defender in some markets, are small Gunpla that are designed to be cute representations of bigger, well-known designs. SD model kits began in earnest in the late '80s following highly popular gashapons and have even been animated into several comedic OVAs and a long-running series.

■ INSTRUCTION SYMBOL GUIDE

Gunpla kits come with very easy-to-follow instruction sheets. Even though the directions can be followed in any language, there are some symbols that it helps to be familiar with.

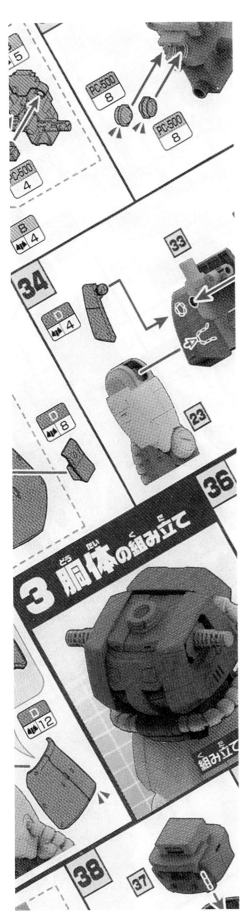

 Decal number

 Use glue

 Sticker symbol

 Do on both sides

 Pay attention to part orientation

 Do not overtighten

 Pieces go on opposite sides

 Repeat this many times

 Do this first

 Do this last

 Turn piece this many degrees

 Optional parts

 Cut

 Opposite sides move parallel

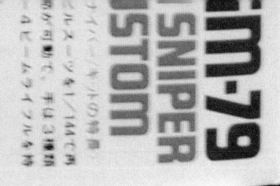

Gm-79 SNIPER CUSTOM

1/144 SCALE MS バリエーション No.3

YMS-09
PROTO TYPE DOM

YMS-09 プロトタイプドム

BANDAI PLASTIC MODEL KIT MADE IN JAPAN
0001308

1/144 SCALE MS バリエーション No.7

MS-14C
GELGOOG CANNON

MS-14C ゲルググキャノン

BANDAI PLASTIC MODEL KIT MADE IN JAPAN
0001318

1/144 SCALE MS バリエーション No.6

MS-06M
ZAKU MARINE TYPE

MS-06M 水中用ザク

MOBILE SUIT
GUNDAM 機動戦士 ガンダム
MOBILE SUIT VARIATION
MSV No. 12
BANDAI

1/14

ZA

MS

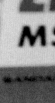

MOBILE SUIT
UNDAM 機動戦士 ガンダム
MOBILE SUIT VARIATION
MSV 30

1/144 SC
RX-78
P
GU

■ GUNPLA HISTORY
x Nick McLean

The history of model kits and toys in Japan is rich and particularly interesting. Who would believe that the world's largest toy company had been started by a one-eyed war veteran, or that Shizuoka was settled by craftsmen and woodworkers?

This essay is based partially on hearsay, and is in no way official or even completely researched. We include it only to share some of the great facts, stories, and rumors about the origin of our hobby.

Pre-Gundam

In 1973, the anime world was changed forever when Bandai released the very first Jumbo Machinder*: the Mazinger Z. Priced at ¥2,650 ($40 USD), the giant toy sold approximately 400,000 units in 5 months. During the same time, Bandai released a replica of the Kamen Rider belt. Both toys exceeded their respective sales expectations. These were the first "character" toys and together they started something revolutionary in the industry.

In the following year, the very first Chogokin (also a figure of the Mazinger Z) was released. With a cost of ¥1300. 500,000 were sold in a year. These sales led to a boom in die-cast character figures that continues even today in the form of Bandai's "Soul of Chogokin" line.

Even with the popularity of the Jumbo Machinder and the Original Kamen Rider belt, these toys were seen as a fluke by the industry, and so character models were not considered a serious business venture. However, this would all change in 1977, thanks to an upcoming anime series.

In 1977, the popularity of the Jumbo Machinder: Mazinger Z caused Bandai to branch out of their current market and export it to the USA under the name Shogun Warrior. Within a year it had sold over one million units. Around the same time, a new anime called *Space Battleship Yamato* (more commonly known as Star Blazers in the west) was beginning to take the world by storm, and it gained a wide audience for its mature themes.

Eager to repeat the sales success of their Jumbo Machinder, Bandai jumped on all anime properties. With the subsequent popularity of *Space Battleship Yamato*, Bandai released a toy-like model of the titular ship with a wind up mechanism and wheels, to appeal to young children. Unfortunately, the sales were not noteworthy.

The popularity of *Space Battleship Yamato* increased due to its rebroadcasting, and Space Battleship Yamato clubs sprung up across Japan. Upon seeing popularity rise again, the creators decided to edit several TV episodes into a full-length feature film.

Against the odds, the new *Yamato* full-length feature sold over two million tickets. This new cultural phenomenon

---

Jumbo Machinder is the name of a series of large-scale plastic robots sold by Bandai's character toy subsidiary, Popy in the 1970s. Although a trademarked brand name, in common usage Jumbo Machinder is often applied to any large-size robot toy rotocast out of polyethylene terephthalate (PET), a sturdy plastic also used for shampoo bottles.

Jumbo Machinders are generally (but not always) 24" in height. After Popy's success with the Jumbo Machinder series, several other Japanese companies, including Takatoku, Nakajima, and Clover began producing large-size plastic robot toys as well. Several of the Jumbo Machinders were retooled for sale in the USA in the late 1970s as Shogun Warriors.

Hobby Japan is a Japanese hobby magazine and publishing company, which specializes in roleplaying, war, and tabletop games. They also focus on action figures, toys, and artbooks for successful anime, manga and light novel franchises.

CROWN MODEL ROBOT SERIES

鉄人28号

★ゼンマイ付★

© 光プロダクション　横山光輝

Tetsujin 28 was of the first mecha to be available as a model kit, often including motors and wind up gimmicks, typical of the time.

outsold even Star Wars in Japan. Anime fever had begun. Following the theatrical release of *Yamato*, Bandai witnessed a huge surge in its sales for the Yamato kit.

In December of that same year, the first character model featured in Hobby Japan* magazine was released.

The featured character model was none other than the scale replica of the Space Battleship Yamato released by Bandai.

What made this issue a landmark and of influential relevance to Gunpla is the fact that the article featured advanced techniques pertaining to modifying the kit itself, and removing the unrealistic toy mechanisms. Suddenly consumers saw that these character model kits could be improved, or modified to a different design. This issue of Hobby Japan flew off the shelves, and set a Hobby Japan sales record for the time; at the same time, Bandai's Yamato kit also made record sales.

It was with this final success of Bandai's Yamato model kit, that other toy manufacturers realized the viable business potential in marketing products linked to anime and TV licenses. They began sponsoring the production of anime series, and created a boom in super robot TV shows and toys throughout the late 70s and 80s.

Freedom Fighter

Following the smash hit of *Space Battleship Yamato's* theatrical release, the majority of toy companies across Japan began contacting anime studios to sponsor shows in exchange for toy and marketing rights.

This, of course, limited the full potential of the creativity that the studios were allowed to exercise. It was a time where toy companies dictated what could be produced and sponsorship could be withdrawn without warning. This would later prove to be a fatal flaw in the case of the original Mobile Suit Gundam.

In the late 1970s, a toy company by the name of Clover approached Sunrise Studios to begin producing a new show. The original concept was called "Freedom Fighter" and at the time did not include a giant mecha robot.

The original concept proposed by Sunrise revolved around a group of young boys and girls growing up on a warship named Battlestar Pegasus during an unspecified conflict. The Battlestar Pegasus would eventually evolve into the famous White Base icon from Mobile Suit Gundam.

After reviewing the original concept, Clover requested a few changes to be made. One of them was from Clover's president, who gave a direct order to include a robot. Due

to this, a decision was made to relegate the initial concept storyline to a minor plot in the new series. It was determined that the new series would revolve more around the robot than the original children.

The actual design of the White Base was then recycled from the cutting room floor of Daitarn 3 (a previous project which Tomino and Okawara worked on.)

Tomino and Okawara would later lament their decision to use this design as the ship, which seemed out-of-place when compared to the more militaristic vessels in MS Gundam.

As for the famous robot design that would be known as Gundam, Takachiho Haruka, a member of Studio Nue, recommended the power suits described in Robert A. Heinlein's Starship Troopers as the basis for their robot designs.

Kunio Okawara initially

designed infantry inspired robot suits that were 2.5m tall, but at the last minute Clover (who was more used to working with Super Robots*) wanted to change the robots to be 100m tall in order to be more appealing to children.

The designers at Sunrise and executives at Clover discussed at great length the size of the robots. Though it seemed the smallest that Clover would concede was 50m, finally Sunrise was able to convince them to settle at 18m.

Due to the realistic intent of the production staff, three early "power suits" were designed: one for close range combat, one for mid-ranged, and a final for long-ranged combat. These would become the Gundam, Guntank, and Guncannon respectively.

It was at this time that the staff dropped the name "power suit" and switched it to "mobile suit" to avoid any possible property infringement with the novel.

The setting for the new show was originally planned to take place in space stations. However, a staff member working on the project provided information on O'Neill Cylinders (O'Neill colonies)*.

It was then decided that these colonies were better suited for the setting, due to their size, which allowed for fighting both inside and outside.

Super Robot is a term used in manga and anime to describe any giant robot, (or mecha) with an arsenal of fantastic super-powered weapons, and extreme resistance to damage unless the plot calls for it. This is distinct from Real Robots, which are portrayed as used by military organizations in the same manner as tanks or aircraft.

An O'Neill cylinder (also called an O'Neill colony) is a design for space settlement proposed by American physicist Gerard K. O'Neill. The concept of which was first shown in his 1976 book The High Frontier: Human Colonies in Space.

Yoshiyuki Tomino is a Japanese mecha anime creator, animator, director, screenwriter and novelist. He is best known for creating the Gundam anime franchise.

Charles Bronson was an actor. He starred in films such as Once Upon a Time in the West, The Magnificent Seven, The Dirty Dozen, The Great Escape, Rider on the Rain, The Mechanic, and the Death Wish series. He was often cast in the role of a police officer, gunfighter, or vigilante in revenge-oriented plot lines.

Another last-minute change was the main colours of the main robot, titled "Gundam". Initially, the Gundam was coloured in realistic shades of gray. However, Clover felt that the colours would not stand out on a shelf next to other toys, and requested the now famous red, white, blue, and yellow colours.

Along with the major changes to the plot of the show, the tentative title "Freedom Fighter" would be swapped for "Gunboy". From there it became *Gundam*, a name that would be widely known.

There are several stories for how the name Gundam came about, but the best story is how Gundam wouldn't be Gundam without Charles Bronson.

The Bronson Connection

In 1978, a movie based on US Truckers, called *Convoy*, was released in Japan. Grossing approximately 14.3 million USD in sales, it was a smash

"Villain of the Week" (or, depending on genre, "monster of the week", "freak of the week" or "alien of the week") is a term that describes the nature of one-use antagonists in episodic fiction. The main characters usually confront and vanquish these characters, often leaving them never to be seen again (as in Scooby Doo).

Char Aznable is a fictional character from the Gundam franchise. He was originally one of the main antagonists in Mobile Suit Gundam and later became one of the protagonists of Mobile Suit Zeta Gundam. He is best known for being the archenemy of the first Gundam pilot, Amuro Ray.

hit in Japanese theatres. After abandoning the initial "Freedom Fighters" title, Sunrise's project director Yoshiyuki Tomino* changed it to "Gunboy", a play on Convoy with a Japanese accent.

Unfortunately, when this name was submitted to Clover, it was met with criticism. It was then that the team began to search elsewhere for inspiration, and it came from the most unlikely of sources.

In the 1970's, the actor Charles Bronson* was an icon in Japan, due to the huge popularity of his films. In 1978, Mandom, an upcoming men's cosmetic brand, paid a then-ridiculous sum of ¥20 million to secure Charles Bronson's services for television and print ads. The TV spot featured him smiling smugly in a bar before saying, 'Mmmmmmm.... Mandom'.

This is easily one of the first and most hysterical cases of celebrity endorsements in Japan ever.

However, it was a huge success and Mandom captured 98% of their market share, putting Mandom on the bodies and lips of the men of Japan. One of whom was Yoshiyuki Tomino.

It was most likely the case, due to the release of Mandom, that one day after seeing too many Mandom ads, the previously-rejected title of Gunboy fused with Mandom to become *Gundam*. But the explanation

given to Clover at the time was a merging of "Gunboy" and "Freedom"

Original Reception and Cancellation

Kidou Senshi Gundam first aired on April 7, 1979 across Japan, and had respectable launch ratings.

As the show progressed, it began to steadily slump in its ratings. It was for this reason that during production, Clover requested a "monster of the week"* format which led to the addition of popular designs, such as the Gouf and Dom mobile suits. Yet even with these new additions, the ratings continued to slip. In a panic, the order for more monster like mecha was placed, and enormous Mobile Armors were forced to appear in the show. Unfortunately, the ratings' fall continued.

With the declining ratings, product sales also slowed. Clover had experienced record sales with their Gundam, but their profits were still beneath their high expectations. However, a fan base began to slowly grow. Fan mail, mostly from teenagers and women, started reaching the production crew, protesting a lack of the character Char Aznable* and more serious subject matters.

The slowly-growing audience could not catch up in time, and Clover gave the order to cancel

Gundam's production while the show was still airing. The original 53-episode storyline would be condensed into 43, and even that was only because Sunrise successfully argued for a slight extension.

It was during this time that reruns of Mobile Suit Gundam began to air during different time slots, even though the original show was still being produced. As Gundam entered its rebroadcasting, it slowly gained popularity. By the end of its run, Gundam had an average audience rating of 10% in most areas, going as high as 29% in other areas. A cover article in Animec* magazine built interest in the series, and critical response to the female characters was particularly strong. Clover took notice of this resurgence of popularity and realized they had made a mistake in cancelling the show.

As Gundam's original run came to a close, Clover desperately wanted to get it back on the air, but it was too late to undo their decision to cancel.

Instead, in September 1979 the G-Armour* appeared in the show at the request of Clover. Determined to make a profit, Clover released the Gundam DX Union combiner set, a knock-off Robo Union toy, with anticipations of high sales for the holiday season.

Unfortunately, the DX Union was a disaster, and despite Clover asking Sunrise to extend the show in order for them to sell New Year's toys, it was too late. The decision for Gundam's cancellation was final. In hopes for a future franchise, Clover requested that Amuro Ray, the main character who was scripted to die in the final episode, instead survive in case a sequel was ever necessary Despite their best efforts, Gundam ended on schedule.

Origin of Gunpla

Toy sales were not doing as well as expected as the show began airing. To help compensate for the weak toy sales, Sunrise suggested that Clover manufacture character model

kits featuring Gundam suits.

Clover's response was simple. They did not believe the slump could be helped by simply increasing the amount of products for characters that already didn't sell. Sunrise still saw value in their idea and demanded the consent to approach another manufacturer to make model kits, and surprisingly enough, Clover agreed. Sunrise approached Aoshima*, known today for their car model kits.

At this time, Aoshima had released many mecha kits before Gundam was released. One of their more popular and noted model lines was called Union Robo. Marketed as an original character design, the Union Robo line was a series of combiner model kits that could be combined together to form larger robots. Unsurprisingly, the line was exceedingly popular.

In 1975, Aoshima won an award from the Kansai Model Retailer's Union for garnering the most sales in the region with their original character model Atoranja and the Union Robo line. The Union Robo line would go on to include many licensed properties. Due to this success with character model kits, Sunrise approached Aoshima first to produce the Gundam model kits and help pay for production of the project.

In retrospect, we may all be

Animec is one of the first Anime Magazines published around 1980-81. It was released due to the popularity of Space Battleship Yamato, and it's 1st issue sold millions of copies during it's first release.

During the One Year War, the RX-78 Gundam had a design drawback in terms of mission versatility. To correct this problem, the Earth Federation designed the **G-Modules** as various support parts for the Gundam in the form of G-Parts A and B. The G-Armor is the combination of both G-Parts A and B with the whole

Gundam mobile suit.

Aoshima Bunka Kyozai Company Limited is a well-known Japanese model car, model aircraft and model ship manufacturer that specializes in plastic unassembled models. They are one of the oldest model companies in Japan, being founded in Shizuoka by a craftsman selling wooden models before World War II.

Lalah Sune is a main character from Mobile Suit Gundam.

The first 1/144 Gunpla.

amazed that Aoshima declined involvement, however at the time, *Gundam* was simply just another under-produced anime property attached to a shaky minor toy company.

Sotsu, the creators of the Space Battleship Yamato kits, had previous success with Bandai in manufacturing their Yamato model kits and recommended them to Sunrise as a viable alternative.

Bandai initially turned Sunrise down as well, but with the financial intervention of the Sotsu Agency, Bandai agreed to produce the kits.

By now, the decision to cancel *MS Gundam* had been made, and the show was already shortened to 43 episodes. As a result, the very first Gundam kits were released six months after the cancellation of the show (but well into its successful rebroadcasting.) Sales were explosive, leading to an all-time high for the sale of a character model kit, and thus the Gundam Boom began.

The Gunpla Boom

Gunpla first appeared on the market in July 1980, with the original 1/144 scale Gundam for ¥300. It is estimated that up to 7 million units of the kit were sold. Priced far cheaper than the tin toys sold by Clover, the model kit was a sensation.

Riding this wave of popularity, in October 1980 work began on a film adaptation of the series, changing the story to be slightly more adult-themed, omitting filler stories and some of the more ridiculous-looking weapons and enemies.

Since the *Space Battleship Yamato* compilation movie had enjoyed such big success, renewing life for its toys and tie-ins, the Gundam movie was also compiled and then stretched into three parts. The first part was released in cinemas on March 14th, 1981, with a special event screening on February 22 in Shinjuku, Tokyo called the Anime New Century Declaration. Thousands of teenagers showed up to the screening, some dressed like the characters Char Aznable and Lalah Sune*.

Just in time for the film's wide release, the March 1981 cover of Hobby Japan was comprised of all Gundam, and the issue sold out immediately. Books compiling Hobby Japan articles were released as How to Build Gundam and How to Build Gundam 2. These books contained within them the original modified kits that would later inspire the Mobile Suit Variation (MSV) line.

This was the first time a publisher saw an explosive sales effect directly resulting from its affiliation to the Gunpla Boom. Yoshiyuki Tomino would further go on to capitalize off this opportunity, producing a three-part Gundam novelization, which ended up selling 50 million copies in Japan alone.

By this time, Aoshima, no doubt realizing their mistake, attempted to market another mecha character model called Ideon. However, it came a little too late and they were unable to recover their lost market shares.

The second Gundam compilation film, *Soldiers of Sorrow*, was released on July 11, 1981 and the final part of the trilogy, *Encounters in Space*, was released on March 13, 1982.

Encounters in Space made a record 1.29 billion yen at the box office, and the film's ending theme song ("Meguriai Encounters", sung by Inoue

Daisuke) was also the first anime song to chart in Japan's pop charts. This began the trend of incorporating pop music in anime. Following the success of the third Gundam movie, Bandai released the Real Type 1/100 Gundam line in April 1982.

Gunpla Backlash

The Gundam Boom was not all positive, however. Demand for the kits far outstripped supply, to the extent that on January 24, 1982, at a toy shop in Tokyo, 250 elementary and junior high school students stampeded at the release of the 1/100 Gyan. 4 children were seriously injured from being pushed down an escalator, and dozens more had less-severe injuries.

Such events became major headlines across Japan, and Bandai's business ethics came into question. A shortage of stock was blamed, and suspicions and criticisms were leveled at Bandai, accusing them of deliberately planning to create such high demands for their kits. In reality, Bandai production staff was already on a 24-hour-a-day schedule, and the supposed "bad business practices" and shortages were due to a legitimate surge in sales during the holiday season and limitations in the molding technology of the time. It got so extreme that retailers were forced to take ads in newspapers to declare they had no Gunpla

in stock!

By May 1982, Gunpla was receiving a different kind of negative publicity. Now it was being blamed for a string of fires erupting around japan, which was due to unintended equipment being used by children to modify the kits. At the time, modelling magazines were featuring techniques that used heat to melt plastic on the kits to create a more realistic look to the battle damage. These articles were so popular that they were featured on a monthly basis.

Between the months of March and May of 1982, due to the popularity of this type of modification, there were over 25 serious incidents of children building accidentally starting fires while building Gunpla.

Often, paints and cement would be nearby and cause the fires to become uncontrollable. Some of the fires unfortunately lead to deaths, and the media attempted to portray Gunpla as a dangerous hobby to youth. Given time, though, hostilities died down, and by 1983 fans were demanding more Gundam.

Plamo Kyoshiro

Comic Bon Bon (published from 1981-2007) was the venue for a large variety of mecha anime tie-in manga. Popular Comic Bon Bon series included *Aura Battler Dunbine, Armored*

Trooper Votoms, Galactic Drifter Vifam, Heavy Metal L-Gaim, Mobile Suit Gundam MS Senki, Mobile Suit Zeta Gundam, Mobile Suit Gundam ZZ, and many more.

Appearing early in the life of Comic Bon Bon, *Plamo Kyoshiro* was one of its first runaway hits. The title is a play on words: Plamo is a portmanteau of PLAstic MOdels, and "plamo-kyo" literally means 'plastic model fan(s)'. The main character of the manga is named Kyoshiro, hence, *Plamo Kyoshiro.* The story revolves around a young group of plamo-kyo who follow Kyoshiro.

Here is a brief synopsis of the first chapter: after rushing out of school to purchase the latest Gundam model kit, Kyoshiro gets into an argument with some classmates. It nearly turns into a brawl, but before it can go too far, the owner of the hobby shop manages to pull the kids apart. He convinces them to go home and build their kits, and compete in a virtual reality simulation against each other.

All the children return home, where Kyoshiro hastily puts together his RX-78-2. Meeting back at the hobby shop, they sit in front of the large machine and duel each other, just as though they were in the *Gundam* anime. Kyoshiro manages to

defeat his nemesis' Zaku II, but finds that the battle damaged both their precious kits, forcing them to learn and build new kits throughout the series in a never-ending attempt to one-up each other.

The series would be considered unusual today, as it includes not only licensed Gunpla kits, but various other sci-fi vehicles, mecha and even real-life scale models such as tanks. While the series is a fantastical take on mecha modeling, it realized the dreams of so many young plamo-kyo: the idea of piloting your own model kit in a non-fatal battle. Its popularity endured for four years before launching multiple spin-off series' that further the adventures and conflicts of Kyoshiro and his friends.

Plamo Kyoshiro was essentially the heart and origin of Gunpla culture, and the course it ran over the next two decades. While there is unfortunately no official or fan-made translations available, it is still worth viewing if possible even just to see the first appearances of the Perfect Zeong and other MSV classics. Its influence can still be felt even today, as it provided the basic premise for the Sunrise OVA Gunpla Builders Beginning G (2010) and Gundam Build Fighters (2013), which keeps the spirit of Gunpla, and reintroduces many old designs to young mecha modelers today.

MSV Line

The impact of Plamo Kyoshiro on Gunpla culture was profound. As the Real Type kit line succeeded at retail, the manga was introduced and popularized many new designs, most notably the Gundam MSV kit line, released in 1983.

The original MSV (Mobile Suit Variation) series was masterminded by the modeling collective Stream Base, who had two members which were also active in the writing collective Craft-DAN, who authored Plamo Kyoshiro.

The two men, Masahiro Oda and Masaya Takahashi, worked with author Hisashi Yasui and artist Koichi Yamato to produce storylines which would introduce and promote new designs, which would be turned into kits. This lead to the production of not only the MSV line, but BB Senshi (Super Deformed, or SD) and the Musha* series of Gundam kits and media properties.

After the release of the theatrical films, the demand for new designs grew beyond the source material, and Bandai began releasing model kits for Mobile Suits that didn't appear in the original series. This idea of an expanded universe being used to sell products was a big gamble, but luckily it paid off. Despite their success, demand was so high that Bandai was desperate for new Gunpla,

and at one point even a 1/100 Juaggu was planned.

Gundam books were also quite popular at this time, and Kunio Okawara was asked to do some Zaku sketches for a new artbook. He made many different variations, such as the Zaku Cannon and Zaku Marine Type. The sketches were so well-received that Bandai, still desperate for ideas, decided to turn it into the Mobile Suit Variation product line.

In April 1983, the MSV line came to market with three 1/144 products, the Zaku II High Mobility, the Zaku Cannon, and the Prototype Dom. With the success of these kits, new designs from Stream Base/Craft Dan were incorporated into the MSV line, with a new MSV being introduced into the manga at least once month, building up hype for the upcoming MSV kit release.

It was a great system of cross promotion, and continued until December 1984, with the release of the first ever system injection* Gunpla: the 1/100 MSV Perfect Gundam.

Zeta Gundam

While Bandai was enjoying success through their model kits, Clover, having only

Musha Gundam is one of the main Mobile Suits from the series Plamo-Kyoshiro, which then started a separate franchise, the first of which was SD Sengokuden Musha Shichinin Shuu Hen.

YMS-09 PROTOTYPE DOM

MOBILE SUIT GUNDAM/MOBILE SUIT VARIATION No.3 YMS-09 PROTOTYPE DOM

One of the first MSV kits, the Prototype Dom is still in production and can be bought today.

series began with the idea that the main mecha of the show would be the "Zeta" Gundam. Production requested several designers to submit concepts for the upcoming Zeta Gundam mobile suit. Several notable mecha designers, such as Mamoru Nagano* and Kazumi Fujita*, submitted concept designs for the Zeta Gundam. However, it was decided that Kazumi Fujiita's Zeta concept would be used instead of Nagano's.

Nagano had experience working with director Tomino on other anime such as *L-Gaim**, and his designs for both the Rick Dias and Galbaldy Beta mobile suits were accepted into the show. However, Nagano's Zeta Gundam concept would be later retooled into a design called the Hyaku Shiki, which

System Injection *is the name Bandai uses for its patented multi-colored molding technology, where different parts on the same runner are moulded in different colours.*

Mamoru Nagano *is a Japanese manga artist, animator, fashion designer, and mecha designer. He is noted for his work with anime studio Sunrise, primarily due to Heavy Metal L-Gaim*

Kazumi Fujita *is a Japanese mecha designer, who has worked on several anime series and video games, notably Mobile Suit Zeta Gundam, The King of Braves GaoGaiGar Final, and Quo Vadis 2.*

Heavy Metal L-Gaim *is an anime television series which began in 1984 and was directed by Yoshiyuki Tomino. It was the first major project that Tomino and Nagano collaborated on, and was an example of the real robot genre.*

released a dozen toys under the Gundam franchise, quietly went bankrupt with liabilities totalling nearly 1.5 billion Yen.

Vifam, Xabungle, Dunbine and *L-Gaim* were new mecha anime created to compete with Gundam, but all failed to capture the attention of Gundam fans. Naturally, their respective sales were below expectations. It soon became evident that a new Gundam show was needed, thus in 1984 production began in earnest. There would be a new Gundam series.

Production of the new Gundam

came to be very popular.

Initially, there were concerns that the Hyaku Shiki looked too much like a Gundam and would be indistinguishable from the main mobile suit of the show, so to differentiate it, they decided to colour it in a bright gold coating.

Nagano, bitter about not having his design for the Zeta chosen, left the project for many months as it entered production.

Zeta Gundam first aired in March 1985 and was a sensational hit. The reception of Zeta on television set audience viewership ratings records, which to this date are unmatched by any Gundam series.

Even now, Zeta Gundam is regarded as a must-see in the Gundam world and has ardent fans. In fact, as of this writing, Zeta Gundam has recently received its own Real Grade model.

As the show ran, the Zeta Gundam model kit line launched in April 1985 with the 1/144 Gundam RX-178 mk II and the 1/144 Hi-Zack at ¥500 each.

The Zeta Gundam kits were a step up from the old Gundam kits, and featured the revolutionary poly cap joint system. Bandai had used poly caps for the first time on the Vifam line of kits with great

success, and so poly caps would become the standard for all future Gunpla.

Halfway through the production, Tomino approached Nagano and requested he design mobile suits for the finale. Nagano, still sore over losing the Zeta concept to Fujita, disregarded all convention and designed a mobile suit called the Qubeley for the primary antagonist, Haman Karn, as well as the another mobile suit, called the Hambrabi.

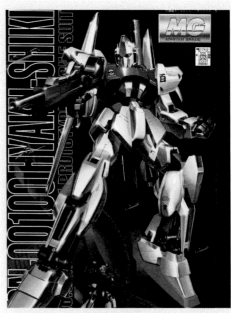

The Master Grade Hyaku Shiki.

Without time to change the design, the Qubeley was used in the show, causing outrage at B-Club (Bandai's important resin garage kit division.) Garage kits were in the height of their popularity, and Nagano's design was very difficult and expensive to cast.

Even with these difficulties, the Qubeley design was a smash hit and Nagano was hired to be the lead designer for the upcoming ZZ Gundam. After designing many concepts for ZZ, he was subsequently fired from the project at the behest of Bandai.

His Qubeley stunt had not gone over well in the boardroom, and he and his ZZ designs were dismissed. In a fury, Nagano swore to never work with Bandai again, and began his own epic manga, Five Star Stories*. Based on his original

vision of L-Gaim, the original mecha featured in Five Star Stories were all designs recycled from his unused ZZ concepts. The Knight of Gold was notably recycled from his earlier design for a Hyaku Shiki MK II.

Even today, Bandai is still not allowed to produce any Five Star Stories products, and a thriving garage resin kit community still exists for these products today.

The End of the Boom

By the end of 1985, despite the popularity of Zeta Gundam, Bandai was experiencing a sharp decline in sales, down to

The Five Star Stories is a manga series created by Mamoru Nagano, which was based on the original plot of Heavy Metal L-Gaim. The story primarily takes place in an alien solar system. The main characters are Lachesis and her husband Amaterasu, who is the god of light and immortal emperor or the Grees Kingdom on the planet Delta Belune.

¥70.7 billion from their ¥84.5 billion in 1984.

Bandai was listed on the Tokyo Stock Exchange in January 1986 to a disastrous effect. The Japanese bubble economy was about to irreparably burst, and with it the Gundam Boom came to a close.

After 1984, Gunpla sales would only ever average half of that of the boom years.

The Golden Era of Gunpla ended gradually, settling into a slump with the rest of the Japanese economy in the '90s. Despite major innovations in molding technology, for Bandai, the original magic and sales have never returned.

World Resurgence

The Gundam franchise officially launched in North America in 1991 with the release of the original Gundam novels (penned by original director Yoshiyuki Tomino.)

However, many fans were introduced to Gundam through a more recent TV series, *Gundam Wing*. The show caused a huge surge in Gundam popularity in the early 2000s, creating a huge fanbase of Gundam enthusiasts.

In just a few years following, *G Gundam*, *Gundam SEED*, and its sequel, *Gundam SEED Destiny*, took to the airwaves. As recently as 2008, *Gundam*

00 started airing on North American networks.

The truth is undeniable: there has been a cultural mecha invasion, not only in North America, but throughout the Western world.

What started with TV shows soon blossomed into merchandise. Though the availability of such merchandise is nowhere near the scale it was during the *Gundam* Wing days, Gundam merchandise is alive and well in the West.

Looking back, it is clear that Gunpla's role in the franchise has been steadily gaining traction since its inception, and its popularity continues to rise in North America and around the world.

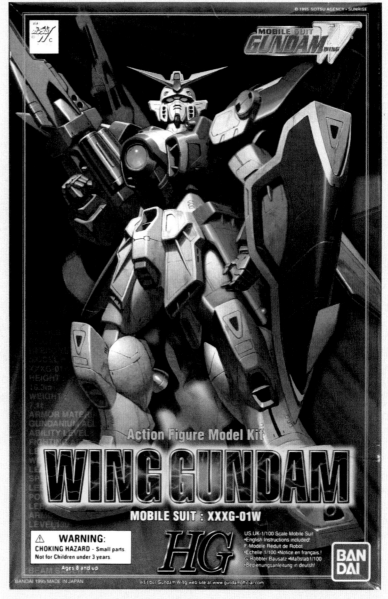

A now-rare US release of the HG Wing Gundam, with English packaging.

TOOLS

So you've gone out and bought your first Gundam model kit, or maybe even received a package from your favorite online store.

Understandably, you might be itching to start building your kit right away.

Before you do, we suggest getting acquainted with the tools you may need to make your building experience that much more enjoyable.

Just like any crafting or design hobby, tools are a necessary part of the modelling experience, and when used properly, your tools will allow you to create a masterpiece.

It's important to note that there are no "bad" tools, and there's always more to learn. What we're covering in this section are simply the "workhorse" tools which you'll come to rely on most often. Learn to use each one to its full potential and you'll be set.

As a final note: take care of your tools and they'll last you quite a while. However, if you don't take proper care of them, you'll find yourself searching for replacements before long.

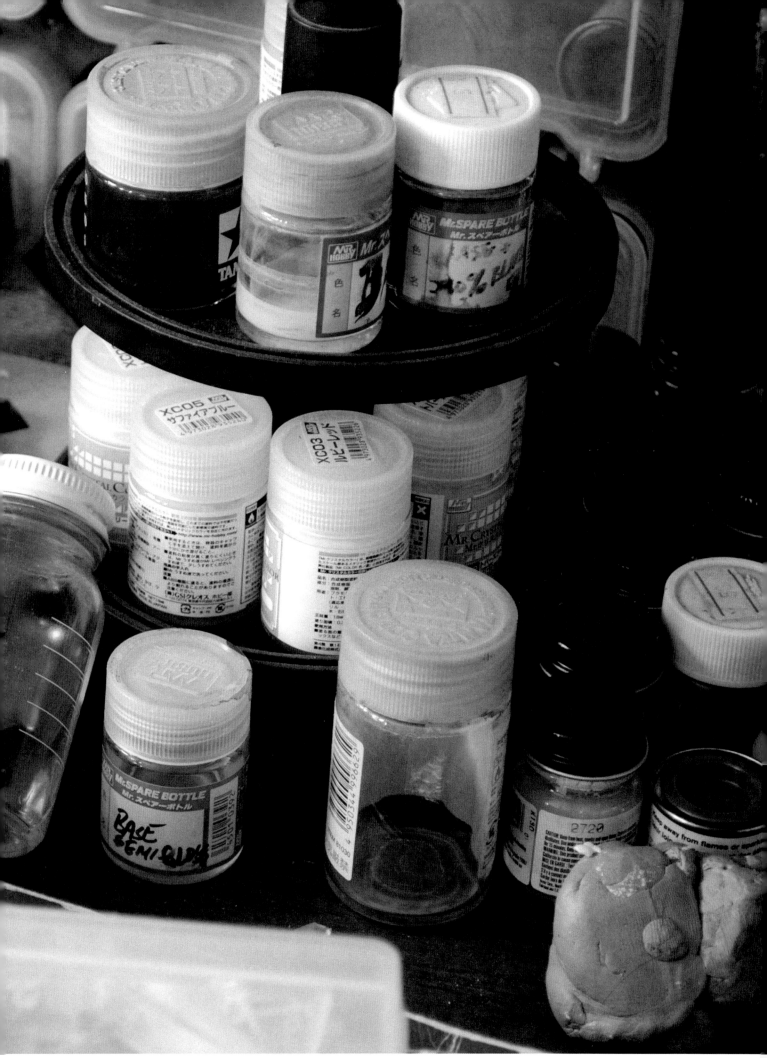

■ KNIVES

One of the essential tools for a model hobbyist is the knife. Knives allow you to cut, carve, and shape plastic into more appealing forms, greatly enhancing a mecha model kit. They can also be used to trim away any and all unsightly nubs. The most common hobby knife available is the No. 11 Exacto Knife. This type of knife has a large blade and very sharp edges, excellent for trimming and cutting. It is also suggested to get an assortment of blades to swap out for different purposes. There are curved blades for softer cuts, as well as saw blades, which can cut large amounts of plastic at once. Both are very useful in modelling.

Note: when cutting plastic or plastic nubs, it is highly recommend to use a cutting mat. Always place the piece on the cutting mat and cut down towards the mat. If you are cutting while holding the piece, please cut away from yourself to prevent injuries.

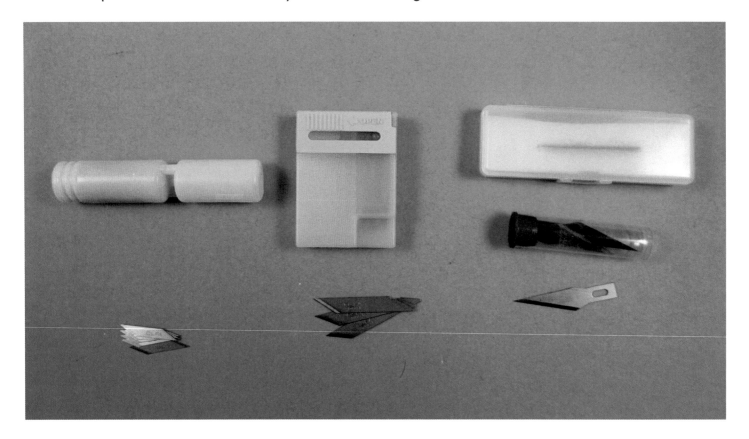

▶ Another knife type commonly used in mecha modelling is the design knife, which comes in different sizes and is much smaller than the No. 11 Exacto Knife.

The smaller blade allows for more control when trimming and cutting, without losing the effectiveness of a sharp blade.

■ SIDE CUTTERS (NIPPERS)

◀ Side cutters are another essential tool for model hobbyists. Similar to pliers and wire cutters, side cutters are used to quickly and easily remove kit pieces from their sprue or runner. There is bevelled edge on one side of the cutting end and a sharp, smooth edge on the other. Each edge can trim and cut many different things, but they work very well for cutting plastic materials.

Model-grade side cutters can be found at many hobby stores. Small wire cutters, often used for crafting and jewelery making, can also be used to cut kit pieces from a runner. They can be found at many discount retailers and arts and crafts stores.

Note: Be aware of your fingers while cutting - getting your skin caught in a side cutter hurts!

■ CUTTING MATS

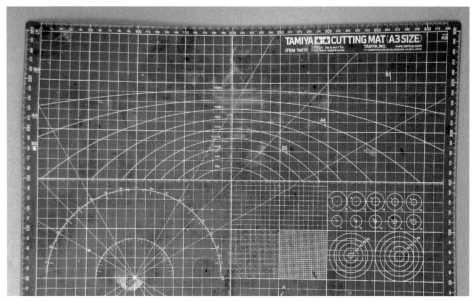

A good cutting mat has a firm surface for the plastic to rest on, as you do not want the plastic to shift or bend as you cut it. Corrugated cardboard and soft, foamy materials do not make good cutting surfaces, given that they are too soft and flexible.

There are cutting mats made specifically for modelling kits. These hobby-grade cutting mats are made of self-healing material, which, over time, can repair damage caused by knives. They are firm and have guidelines for measuring and determining where to properly cut plastic parts and styrene sheets.

▲ Cutting mats are very useful when you are cutting any plastic pieces. They provide a surface to cut down on, without harming the work area. You can use many things as a cutting mat, such as a kitchen cutting board. A piece of thin, non-corrugated cardboard can also suffice.

■ FILES

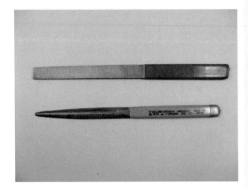

▲ Files can be found in various shapes and sizes. The most common types are regular files, found in hobby stores. These are good for filing small surfaces and different inner shapes, such as squares and circles. The larger files, also known as bastard files, can be picked up in any hardware store. These files are significantly larger and have a blunter grit. They are used to grind straight, long, and smooth surfaces, which a regular file may be too small to handle. They come in various shapes and sizes.

Note: Take care when filing small pieces, as your fingers may protrude out and cause your skin to get filed off.

■ SANDPAPER

▲ Sandpaper is a hobbyist's bread and butter. The important thing to understand about sand paper is the grit number. These numbers are usually denoted on the back of a piece of sandpaper. Common grit numbers are 400 and 600. Lower grit numbers indicate rougher texture, or coarser quality, in the sandpaper. The higher the number, the finer the sandpaper. Sandpaper can go as high as 3000 grit, which is used for polishing.

Other sanding products can be very useful in modelling, as well. One of the drawbacks to using sandpaper is that certain surfaces, such as those on rounded objects, can be difficult to sand. Since so many Gunpla are designed with rounded armor, a sanding sponge or soft sanding sticks/emery boards (often used for fingernails in beauty salons) are recommended for sanding these surfaces. Sanding sponges are readily available at any hardware or automotive store. Sanding sticks can be located in the makeup departments of many stores. Both tools are soft and can conform to any surface to sand away imperfections or seam lines, without greatly effecting the contour of the piece.

■ TWEEZERS

▲ Tweezers are used to handle small pieces, and to apply decals and stickers. They are a very simple tool that can help you pick up and handle small or fine parts that may be difficult to handle with your fingers.

■ SKEWERS, ALLIGATOR CLIPS, AND FOAM

▶ If you are planning to invest a large amount of time in this hobby, you may want to make holders for your pieces, which allow them to easily dry after painting and priming.

To start, take a skewer and wrap a piece of masking tape around the tip so the sticky side faces outward. This will hold plastic pieces for spray painting. Another way is to attach sticky tack, which has enough adhesion power to ensure that the piece stays on the skewer.

The foam is usually leftover styrofoam which can be perforated and used to hold the skewers.

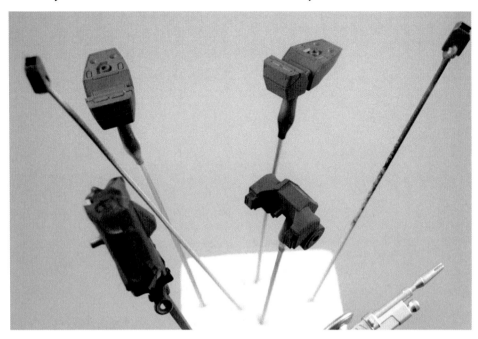

■ BASIC MODELING PUTTY

▶ Modelling putty is another essential tool that allows you to fill gaps and seams in your model kit. You can even sculpt new pieces with a combination of plastic and putty.

The putty used for filling seam lines and gaps comes in a tube, and is usually very soft and has a gel-like consistency.

It eventually hardens into a consistency similar to plastic, but is softer, making it easy to sand. Putties are designed to dry quickly, and will shrink as they dry. The amount of shrinkage depends on the manufacturer's formula.

If you use a putty with high shrinkage to fill a large gap or seam, you must make sure to add enough extra putty to keep it from cracking or depressing into the gap.

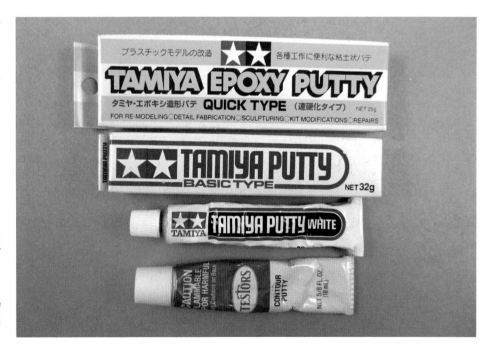

There are different brands of putty, such as Tamiya Grey, Tamiya White, Squadron Green, and Testors Contour Putty. Squadron Green putty can be flakey and must be sanded carefully, as sand paper has been known to rip off large chucks of dried Squadron Green putty.

Note: We suggest wearing gloves when handling putty, as it often contains harmful chemicals.

■ STICKY TACK

▲ Sticky tack is a reusable, pressure-sensitive adhesive that can be found in most supermarkets and hardware stores. It comes in a variety of packages and colors, and is usually sold as a poster-holder. It is malleable, pliable, and can be kneaded or moulded into any shape. It is sticky enough to hold large posters to the wall.

For modelling, sticky tack has two main uses: masking specific patterns, irregularly-shaped objects, and holding small pieces of plastic to skewers for painting. Sticky tack will retain its stickiness even after absorbing a lot of paint pigments. As it absorbs more natural oils from your hand, it becomes stickier and more pliable. This is great for masking, but also causes the tack to lose its original rigidity, which means that it cannot hold heavier objects as well as it could when fresh from the package. Sticky tack becomes more malleable with heat. As the temperature rises in the tack, you can more easily knead and mask with it.

■ GLUE

▶ Glue is another essential tool for modelling, as it binds the plastic pieces to one another.

With nothing to hold them together, models may easily come apart. Glues come in a variety of types, and each type of modelling glue will have its own characteristics. The glues that tend to work best for beginner plastic modelling are:

Polystyrene cement
Cyanoacrylate (super glue)

■ POLYSTYRENE CEMENT

The most common type of glue is known as modelling cement, or polystyrene cement. While each manufacturer has their own formula, most modelling cements can dissolve plastic. When you squeeze two parts together using modelling cement, the plastic pieces will actually bond together.

Once the cement dries, a very strong and solid bond is formed between the two plastic surfaces. This property has made modelling cement a popular choice with modellers.

A major disadvantage to using cement is that when too much is applied, it will completely dissolve through the plastic and damage it. If any glue is dropped or smeared on the surface of the model, it can damage surface details. Modelling cement must be used with care. Do not to put too much cement into holes and cavities that have no exposure to the air, since the cement will not be able to dry properly and will slowly dissolve the surrounding plastic.

Cement glue drying times vary, depending on how much cement is applied and the level of its viscosity. Modelling cement usually comes in three different viscosities: thin, medium, and thick. Very thin formulas will normally dry in seconds, but thick tube cements may take a few hours.

Note: Even when a bond has formed, the plastic may not be fully re-hardened yet, so treat the piece with care for a time.

■ THICK TUBE CEMENT

When scale modelling first became popular, thick tube cement was used almost exclusively. Some model kits from the 1970's and earlier would include a small tube of cement.

The consistency of the thick tube cement is similar to that of toothpaste.

This glue thickness means that it must be used sparingly, to avoid damaging the model kit. Some brands also tend to leave behind a very thin string of glue thread, which can be annoying.

Handling thick tube cement can be a very messy process for beginners, as small amounts may get on your finger tips and inadvertently melt the surface of the model kit.

Although tube cement has lost popularity over the years , it still does have its uses. It is easy to precisely apply small amounts on to small surface areas, and the long drying time allows the modeller plenty of time to position the parts correctly.

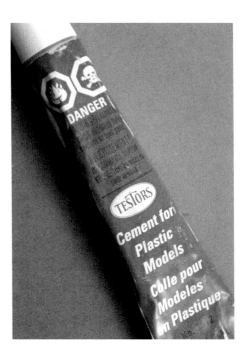

■ ULTRA THIN / LIQUID POLY CEMENT

Ultra-thin cements normally come in small glass bottles with brush applicators fitted into the screw tops.

The consistency of these cements is similar to water. The amount of solvent in them will vary by manufacturer. Before using any cement you are unfamiliar with, test it on a plastic scrap.

Since this glue usually dries quickly, it is less likely to damage parts if accidentally dropped onto the model kit.

The only problem is that you have a limited time to assemble the part, and little time to position the parts, depending on the amount of cement applied.

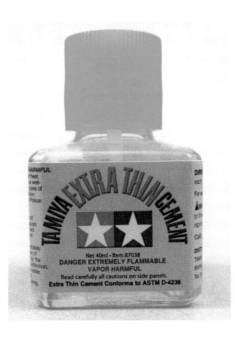

Common brands for polystyrene cement include Testors, Tamiya, Mr. Hobby, and Ambroid. They can be found in any local hobby store.

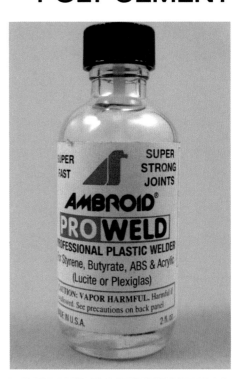

Note: *The thicker the cement, the longer it will take to dry.*

■ CYANOACRYLATE (CA / SUPERGLUE)

▶ This is another tool that is very popular with modellers. Unlike cement, super glue does not dissolve the plastic at all.

Instead, it will adhere to both surfaces and harden, forming the bond by itself. It is very fast-acting and usually dries in minutes to seconds. Handle with care or you will glue your fingers together, or worse yet, glue yourself to your model kit.

If you happen to glue yourself to your model kit with super glue, do not try to pull your skin off of it. Instead, find something with acetone in it, such as acetone-based nail polish remover. Don't just pour it on, since acetone will melt plastic materials. Instead, brush it on and slowly pull your skin away from the model kit

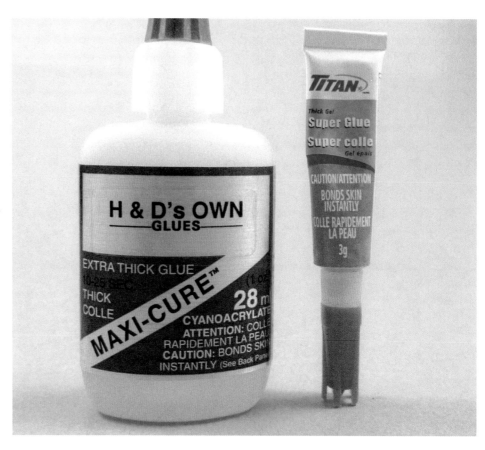

Super glue is good for quick glue jobs and can hold almost anything together, but can also become brittle and break apart easily. Although super glue will stick most things together, the quality of the surface it's applied on is very important.

Any dust or grease on the surface will substantially reduce the bonding strength. Rough surfaces stick together better than smooth ones, so light sanding of the plastic pieces is recommended before gluing.

If you accidentally spill super glue on the wrong surface, it should be immediately wiped off with a paper towel. Any excess that is left to harden must be scraped off with a sharp knife, as it will dry into a very hard state.

Because super glue dries so quickly, make sure you cover the bottle opening once you have applied it. This will prevent the super glue from drying up before you can use it.

Just like the cements, super glue comes in three different types: thick, medium, and thin. The only difference between the three is the viscosity and drying times.

The thicker the CA glue is, the longer the drying time, whereas thinner glue will dry faster. Before buying CA glue, make sure to read about its type and drying time.

For beginners, we recommend using thick-to-medium viscosity glue, which gives you time to reposition the pieces.

Super glue is easily available in your local hobby and hardware stores.

■ MARKERS

▲ Markers can be used for many different purposes in the world of modelling, with the most prominent being panel lining and marking.

Panel lining is using a pen to lightly brush the details on to a Gunpla kit, which will make the finished product 'pop'.

For panel lining, it is recommend you use a paint-based marker, as felt or fine-lining pens will often fade to purple.

"Marking" is when you use a pen to draw areas on the model, a sheet of paper, or styrene to determine where to cut, modify, or sand away.

Gundam Markers are a specific brand of paint markers owned and produced by Bandai, meaning that they're tailor-made for Gundam and Gunpla enthusiasts.

Gundam Markers come in three different categories: Gundam Marker Regular, Real Touch Marker, and the Weathering Marker Set.

■ GUNDAM MARKER REGULAR

▲ These markers are often individually bought and come in two sizes: regular and fine.

The larger-sized, regular Gundam Markers can either be used to paint on their own, or you can extract the ink from them by pressing down on the pen tip and letting the ink inside drip into a mixing cup.

From there, you can thin the ink with alcohol to hand-paint with. These markers come in a variety of colors, and are great for touching-up areas where you cut the pieces from the runner.

The smaller, finer Gundam Markers are for painting panel lines and small crevices. These only come in three colors: black, grey and brown.

Other pens can be used for panel lining, such as Pigmapen, Micro, Koh-I-Noor, and Rapidograph.

■ WEATHERING MARKER SET

▲ When the paint from these markers dries, it has a soft, pastel-like consistency and can be rubbed to mimic some weathering effects such as dirt, dust or even rust.

■ REAL TOUCH MARKER

▲ These markers resemble Sharpie pens on one end, and a fine-tipped pen on the other. These are used to provide shading details to your model kit. In order to use these pens, you must first spray a flat coat on your model. They do not work on glossy or semi-gloss surfaces, only flat/matte surfaces.

33

MR.
HOBBY

79

Mr.COLOR

光沢
GLOSS

シャインレッド
SHINE RED

PRIM

PAINT & THINNER BASICS

In your modelling career, you may reach a point where you wish to start painting your kits. There are a myriad of paint manufacturers that make many different kinds of paint. Deciding which paints to buy, and when and how to use them, can be very confusing to a beginner.

In this section, we will cover the basic fundamentals of modelling paint and thinner. We will talk about the two types of paints: water-based and oil-based. Hopefully this will help modelling newcomers to avoid mistakes commonly made by beginners.

Please be aware that paint manufacturers do change their formulas and products from time to time, so there is always the possibility that new and improved products have been released after this book was published.

■ PAINT ANATOMY

Paint is made up of three major components: pigment, binder and thinner (also called reducer.) Every manufacturer has their own formula for creating their paints, and each will add their own various ingredients.

Pigment is a dry powder that gives paint its colour. The modeling paints offered by hobby shops generally have finer pigments than similar-looking paints at a discount store or art store. Since model kits are scaled miniatures of their life-size counterparts, finer pigments are needed so as not to obstruct their tiny surface details.

Binder is a colorless, transparent glue that carries and adheres the pigments to the surface of what you're painting. It can be the most confusing part of understanding and using paint. Binder is also the main cause of paint "going bad".

The type of reducer required to thin paint will depend on the manufacturer's formula for creating the paint's binding agent. The most common binders are variations of acrylic polymer resin, typically used for modeling paints.

You may have already purchased paints at the hobby store, and noticed that the labels have the word "acrylic" written on them. The term "acrylic" can be a simplified way to describe the type of binder being used in the paint. Yet in hobby and art stores, the term "acrylic" is used to denote water-based paints. In order to keep things simple, we will use "acrylic" to refer to water-based and alcohol-based paints.

Thinner (sometimes called reducer) is the thinning agent used to adjust paint's viscosity so that it can flow well and be applied easily with a brush or airbrush. It can be either water-, alcohol-, or oil-based.

Many acrylic paints can be thinned out by alcohol or water, depending on the formula used. Oil-based paints, such as Humbrol or Model Masters, can be thinned using mineral spirits.

Because each manufacturer has their own binder formula which dictates the usage of either water-, alcohol-, or oil-based thinner, we recommend using the appropriate thinner for each paint, otherwise your paint can go bad. Ask your local hobby shop if the brand of paint you are buying has its own thinner and cleaning agent.

There are some brands of paints that will work with different thinners. For example, the Tamiya brand of acrylic paint can be thinned with alcohol, Windex, or water. The Humbrol enamel brand paint can be thinned with mineral spirits, Varsol, or lighter fluid.

■ WATER BASED PAINTS

True Water-Based Acrylics

Water-based paints are water soluble, meaning that they can be thinned with water. Manufacturers usually recommend using distilled water for thinning.

Thinning with water won't always be a good idea, depending on what paint brand you are using, so read the bottle label carefully. Acrylic color brands commonly found in art stores, such as Golden or Liquitex, have airbrush-thinning mediums with extra binding agent inside.

There is an irreversible chemical change in the binder's molecular level once the paint has cured, causing the coat to become similar to hard plastic.

It is recommended to use distilled water to thin acrylic paints. Many regions have "hard" tap water, meaning the water has high mineral content.

 Hard water can damage acrylic paint because it contains foreign mineral components that may not be compatible with the paint. If you are not sure about the quality

of the tap water in your area, just buy a jug of distilled water to use. It's better to do that than risk ruining your paint job by using tap water.

True water-based acrylic hobby paints are excellent for brush painting. They tend to run a bit thick, and do take longer to dry compared to alcohol-based acrylic paint. Their coats are very strong after drying.

Good water-based acrylics include Vallejo (Spain), Citadel (France), Master/Reaper series (US), Life Color (Italy), Testor's Model Master Acryl (US), Polly Scale Acrylic (US), and artist supply store variations, such as Golden or Liquitex acrylic colors.

Alcohol-Based Acrylics

Alcohol-based acrylic has alcohol in its thinner as a solvent. It can be washed off with water before it cures, and for hand brushing, it can be thinned with a little water.

Alcohol, such as 99% rubbing alcohol, is most commonly used to thin these paints.

Currently, there are two alcohol-based acrylic paints on market, both of which are from Japan. The first is GSI Creos' (previously called Gunze Sangyo) Aqueous Hobby Color, the second is Tamiya Acrylic Color.

Please note that GSI's Aqueous Hobby Color paint is acrylic, but GSI's Mr. Color paint is lacquer. We would also like to note that GSI's Aqueous Hobby Color is not currently available outside of Asia.

For brush painting, you can thin Tamiya and Aqueous Hobby Color paints with their respective thinners, alcohol, Windex, or water. Each will behave differently depending on which thinner you use, but it is not recommended to thin them with water.

Tamiya Acrylic, which is widely available, is very forgiving for airbrush usage but no so much for hand-painting. This is because alcohol-based acrylic dries fairly quickly, which tends to leave brush marks on the surface.

Note: Alcohol-based Tamiya acrylic thinner is not compatible with True water-based acrylics, like Vallejo or Poly Scale.

■ OIL BASED PAINTS

Enamel Paints

As with water-based acrylics, enamel binder also undergoes a chemical change when drying. The difference is that enamel coating is even harder than acrylic coats.

It is extremely hard once it has completely cured, hence the name "enamel"; it was intended to cure into a state similar to our own teeth.

Because enamel paint has a slow drying time, the surface may at first feel dry to the touch, but under the surface, the paint is still moist.

It's a good idea to wait about 24 hours to handle a piece that's just been painted with enamel.

Due to this slow drying property, enamel paints are more forgiving when hand-brushing, since the time will allow the paint to level on its own and cause the brush strokes to disappear.

When painting with enamel paints, we recommend you use enamel/mineral spirit based thinner. They can be found at your local hobby or hardware store. You can also experiment with other thinners, which have been known to work just as well.

Other thinning agents you can use with enamel paints are Zippo Lighter fluid, Varasol, and any paint thinner that contains mineral spirits.

Lacquer Paints

Lacquer paints, when used in the modelling hobby, can be a challenge. Lacquer paints are very toxic to human health because their solvent contains volatile organic compounds (VOCs). VOCs are toxic and have a high evaporation rate at room temperatures. This causes lacquers to dry extremely fast.

Even though the hobby-grade lacquer paints and thinners are relatively mild when compared to industrial grade lacquers, you should not breathe in their fumes or allow them to come in contact with your bare skin. Before you start painting, make sure you are in an area with good ventilation, and wear a painter's mask.

There is a difference between some hobby-grade lacquers (such as Mr. Color and Gaia Notes) and the industrial grade lacquers you can find at your local hardware store.

The difference is that the some of the hobby-grade solvent is actually alcohol-based, and is in reality a "synthetic" lacquer, while Alclads are true lacquer paints.

Hobby Lacquer paints also come in a spray can. For the purposes of this book we will be using lacquer spray cans, as they are much more economical for a beginner to use.

Some paint spray cans contain enamel paint, so be sure to read the label carefully know what you are purchasing.

Note: *True lacquer thinner is great for cleaning tools, but will completely dissolve most modelling plastic material. Use caution when working with lacquer thinner.*

■ PAINT TYPE COMPARISON

Many modellers have their own preferences on which type of paint to use for which job. There is no "right" way; it all depends on preference and situation.

You can utilize the different characteristics in different paints to achieve your desired results.

Depending on the strength of the solvent used in each paint, modellers should be careful when layering different types of paints on top of each other.

Lacquer has the strongest solvent, followed by enamel, then acrylic water-based. You can apply an acrylic paint over an enamel or lacquer coat, and apply an enamel paint over a lacquer coat, as well.

Never spray or brush lacquer paints over enamel or acrylic coats. The strong solvent in lacquer paints will dissolve enamel and acrylic paint layers.

Even when applying the same types of paint, you should always wait until the first layer has dried or cured completely before laying down the second layer.

If you have already painted an acrylic layer and plan to use enamel paint for washes or panel lining, it is imperative that you protect it with a gloss clear coat beforehand. his way, the enamel paint will not harm the acrylic layer beneath it.

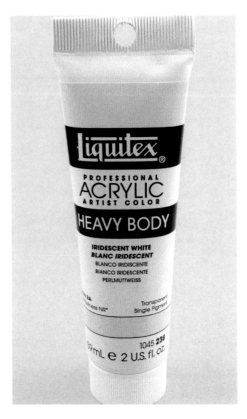

▲ Liquitex and many other water-based acrylics are available in most art and craft stores.

■ Water Based Acrylics

Liquitex, Golden, Model Master Acryl, Vallejo, Citadel, Life Color, Master/Reaper Series, Poly Scale Acrylic, Floquil (new formula)	Pros:	Cons:
• Can be thinned with water and cleaned with alcohol or Windex • Lacquer thinner will react with it, leaving you with disgusting chunks of latex • Recommended if you don't build kits very quickly, are generally careful when handling parts, and if you are starting out with hand-painting	• Non-toxic • Easy to clean up • Good skintone colors for figure painting • Relatively cheap • Many thinner additives available to achieve different effects • Fairly strong coat • Great for hand-brushing	• Poor adhesion compared to oil based • Long curing time; takes a day or more, depending on the weather • need primer to be tough

■ Alcohol Based Acrylics

Tamiya, GSI Aqueous Hobby Color	Pros:	Cons:
• Tamiya is widely available in the USA, but GSI Aqueous Hobby color is difficult to get • Can be thinned with water, but alcohol or Windex is better. Can also be thinned with lacquer thinner • Recommended if you are just starting out	• Non-toxic • Decent curing time (within hours, depending on thinner used) • Lots of great, vibrant colours	• Really poor adhesion; the coat scratches off easily (particularly Tamiya, which needs a top coat to protect it) • Tamiya is poor for hand-brushing, but it can be done • Once paint dries in the bottle, it can't be revived

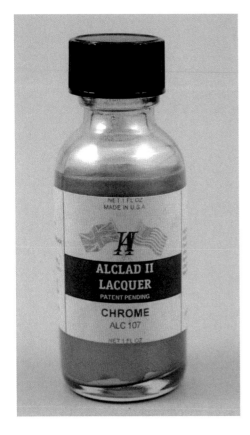

▲ Many lacquer products are difficult to ship overseas. Every country has different regulations on sending and receiving chemicals.

Some Japanese brands, like Finisher's and Gaia Notes, are particularly hard to buy overseas.

■ Lacquers

Floquil (old formula), most automotive paints, GSI Mr. Color, Gaia Notes, Tamiya Spray Cans, Alclad	Pros:	Cons:
• Mainly used for airbrushing. Can be used for hand-painting when using Mr. Retarder to slow the drying process • Mr. Color and Gaia Notes paints can be revived with Mr. Thinner if they dry out • Must be applied in a very well-ventilated area	• Fast drying and curing times (an average of 10 minutes) • Can be good for hand-brushing with Mr. Color leveling thinner, and/or by adding a little Mr. Retarder to Mr. Thinner • Forms a tough film that is stronger than most enamels • Excellent adhesion and very scratch-resistant • Can be revived, even if completely dry, with proper thinner	• Can be expensive • Very very toxic!

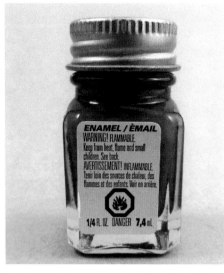

▲ Enamels typically come in smaller quantities than laquer or acrylic paint, however their cost is lower as well.

A modeler starting out will find it much cheaper to buy a variety of enamels than any other paints.

■ Enamels

Testors, Humbrol, Tamiya Enamels, Model Masters	Pros:	Cons:
• Tamiya enamels are not available in North America, but you can get them in Asia • Can be thinned with mineral spirits, like industrial paint thinner, or lacquer thinner, which can decrease drying and curing times	• Cheap • Widely available • Good for hand-painting since it self-levels • Forms a tough coat once dry • Paints will last a long time	• Long drying time; can take days depending on the amount brushed on • Long curing time of at least a day or more • Toxic

■ TOPCOAT FINISHES

As you build and paint your model kit, you will need to protect your work with a final layer of clear coat. This final layer of paint is mostly clear, and dictates the final look of the kit. There are three different kinds of top coating finishes: flat (matte), semi-gloss, and gloss.

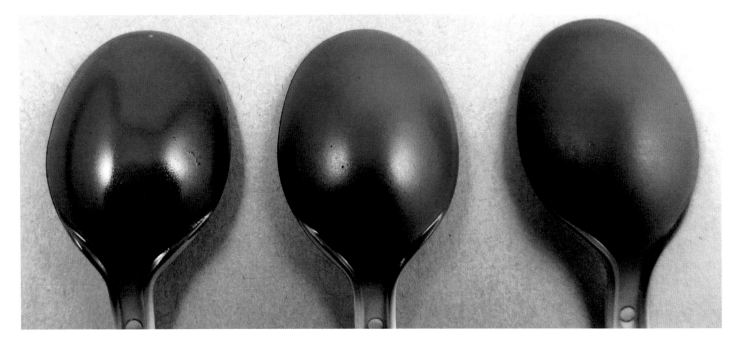

Gloss Top Coat:

This top coat contains no pigments whatsoever. No matter what kind of paint you use, it will give your kit a shiny finish. Depending on how you spray the gloss coat, you can even achieve a mirror shine. This coat type is commonly used on car and motorcycle model kits.

Gloss coats have other uses, as well. They can be used in the intermediary painting process, when you are weathering or before you panel-line. This will help protect the lower layers of paint from damage as you add weathering details, panel lines, or water slide decals.

Semi-Gloss (Satin) Top Coat:

The semi-gloss (satin) or flat (matte) clear coat paints are gloss top coats with tiny particles of frost pigment. The frost pigment provides a rougher surface and helps to disperse light, so that the surface looks dull instead of shiny.

A semi-gloss coat has fewer frost pigments, which give the model kit a look that is neither dull nor shiny. Because of the frost pigments, these coats can only be used as the last coat, after all your paint, panel lines, and decals have been applied.

Flat (Matte) Clear Coat:

The flat and semi-gloss look is very common in military models, as real-life planes and tanks are usually painted in non-reflective paints. But since mecha models are nonexistent, you can finish it with semi gloss or flat coats as you choose.

Note: Top coats are available in many brands, such as GSI, Tamiya, Testors, and Humbrol. These can be found in your local hobby store.

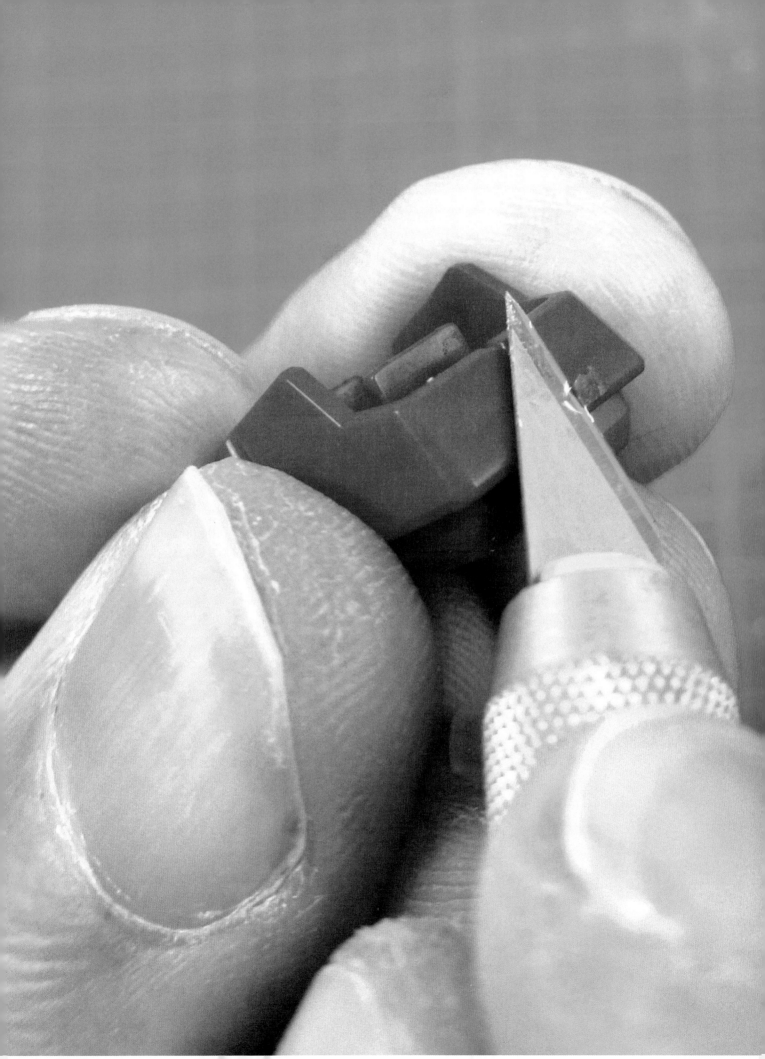

GUNDAM EXIA

✕ ROBERT DAVIDSON

Gundam Exia is one of the main suits in *Gundam 00*, the series responsible for renewing the franchise's popularity after *Gundam SEED Destiny*.

This kit was originally released in October 2007, making it a newer design.

As a general rule, more recent kits have easier cleanup and are a good choice for beginners.

In this chapter, we'll build the Exia step-by-step, and examine the basics of following an instruction manual, nub cutting, and the "adze" technique.

We'll also introduce some basic sanding and spraying techniques. You don't need to invest in an airbrush or expensive gear to start modelling All you need is some effort, and a quick visit to your local hobby or craft shop.

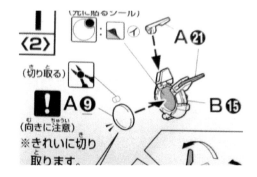

■ HOW TO FIND PARTS

Gunpla manuals are some of the most forgiving in scale modeling. Bandai really makes an effort to make their kit manuals easy to understand, even if you don't read any Japanese.

All of the pieces in the instruction sheet are referenced by a letter and number for identification. The letter refers to the runner label, and the number refers to the part number on that runner.

▲ To look for a piece labeled C25, locate the letter C stamped on the runner, then find piece 25.

▲ Once you've found the piece you are looking for, examine the best way to apply your nippers so the part doesn't get damaged.

▲ Polycap runners don't have a letter, they are referenced by the letters PC.

■ *Cutting Parts From the Sprue*

▲ Method 1: Place the flat part of your nippers up against the side of the piece you wish to remove from the sprue, and cut. The trick is to minimize the amount of nub left on a piece after it's been cut out.

▲ Method 2: Place the flat part of the side cutter in the middle of the connecting plastic. Cut the piece out. You should have a significant amount of nub left sticking out of the piece, giving you more freedom to make a precise cut.

▲ Proceed to cut the nubs off using method #1. This will minimize the amount of discoloration when cutting the piece off the sprue.

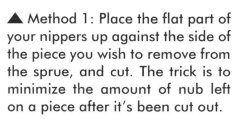

◀ If you can't afford nippers, a pair of good nail clippers is a great substitute. It may be awkward to cut some pieces, but the edge is as good as that on any pair of nippers!

Always use a specific set of nippers for plastic only. Use another pair when cutting resin, vinyl or metal. This keeps your model nippers sharp and ready for action!

■ PREBUILDING TECHNIQUES

Prebuilding a kit is a technique that allows you to fully assemble the model (for better planning of modifications or custom colour schemes), but still be able to take it apart easily.

If you build the kit normally (by following the instructions), you'll find it very difficult to separate the pieces. Prebuilding simply gives you an idea of what it could look like, but still offers flexibility to modify.

▲ Professional quality nippers can cost from $15-100. Many people swear by Tamiya brand nippers.

■ *Peg Cutter Technique*

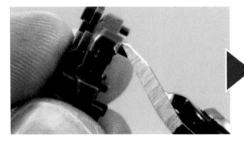

▲ Angle your nippers on the peg and cut. The angle increases the amount of contact area at the end of the piece while shortening it to make it easier to pull apart.

▲ The trick is to shear the pegs on an angle so that they still have just enough tension to hold the piece, but not enough so that the pieces stick together tightly.

▲ Be careful not to cut off too much, or else the pieces won't stay together.

■ *Screwdriver Technique*

▲ Use a screwdriver that is just slightly wider than the hole. Insert it into the hole where the peg will go.

▲ Apply pressure and turn the screwdriver ten to fifteen times. You should see plastic being shaved off as you turn the screw driver.

▲ Do a test-fit. At this stage, the pieces should fit snugly together, but not tight enough that they cannot be separated.

■ CLEANING PARTS

Unfortunately, nippers aren't perfect tools and there will always be some leftover plastic on the pieces you snip out. Not only does this interfere with the appearance of the kit, but even handling the kit can be painful if there are sharp, plastic bits sticking out!

■ *Using a Knife and Cutting Mat*

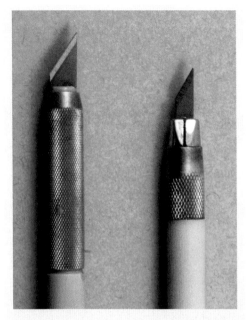

▲ Design knifes are a very useful tool in modeling. With a smaller blade than a regular X-Acto, they are less likely to cut you in a slip.

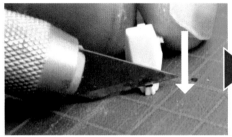

▲ Take a hobby knife and place the piece on a cutting board. Cut downward towards the board, shearing off the nub.

▲ This is a much more accurate method than using the nippers, and should leave no nub marks

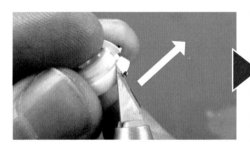

▲ When holding a piece in your hand, expose the nub, take a hobby knife and place it so that the blade is facing away from yourself, but towards the nub.

▲ Cutting one side off first and then rotating the piece for a second cut is very effective.

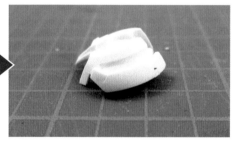

▲ The final piece should show minimal discoloration, and have a smooth surface.

Knives are cool, and so is safety! Ok, maybe not, but cutting your own hand open really isn't cool, either. There is an old adage that says:

It's not a question of if you will cut yourself, but when.

This is quite true in model building, as a modeler is often faced with holding a knife in an awkward position to cut a very small piece.

The best advice is to develop habits that put you at the least risk for cuts. Everyone's hands are shaped differently, so you need to find what is comfortable for you.

Of course, the old standby tips still apply to everyone: Always use sharp blades and never cut towards yourself.

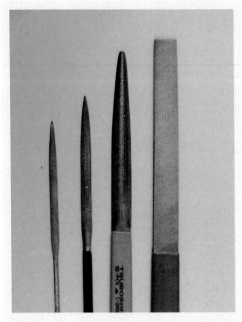

▲ A modeler needs a variety of jewellers' and fine bastard files in his arsenal. Avoid diamond encrusted files, they aren't suitable.

■ Using a File

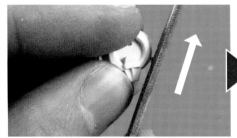

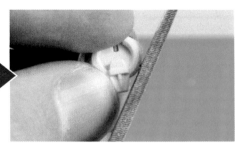

▲ Use the file of your choice to grind, or file, at the nub until smooth. Make sure to grind the file in only one direction.

▲ The forces of pushing and pulling the file while grinding can cause the side of the piece to become rounded slightly.

■ Removing Cut Marks

If you're not planning on painting the entire kit, sometimes white cut marks still show up on the pieces (even if you clean them, as mentioned previously.) Here are some simple steps to getting rid of them.

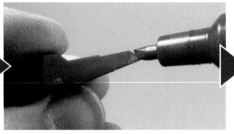

▲ Choose a Gundam Marker or Pigma pen with a colour similar to that of the piece.

▲ Lightly colour the white marks with the pen.

▲ After allowing a few seconds to dry, use a finger, eraser, or cloth to wipe away any excess marker ink.

Gundam Markers can also be applied by brush. Simply press the Gundam Marker, tip-first, into a small paint dish.

Paint will pool around the tip, and can then be brushed onto a model

kit in specific spots, or by using techniques like dry-brushing.

Gundam Markers can also be diluted with Mr. Thinner Lacquer Thinner to make a fast wash.

While Gundam Markers are useful in their own way, they typically produce very thick, dark panel lines. By diluting the Gundam Marker and applying it with a brush, you can achieve a lighter effect.

■ CEMENTING

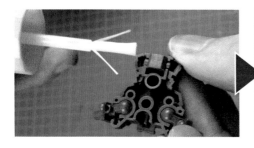

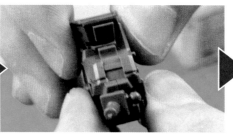

▲ Take the glue and lightly brush it onto all the pieces that will be touching one another when the parts are put together.

▲ Put the pieces together and squeeze tightly so that the cement/ glue oozes out of the cracks.

▲ Different cements take different amounts of time to fully dry. Test your pieces, and if they are strong, you can then proceed to wet-sand away the excess glue.

■ SANDING

The main purpose of sanding is to prepare the plastic surface for coats of paint and primer.

By sanding the piece thoroughly, you also remove unwanted seam lines and any imperfections in the plastic.

You can sand pieces by using two methods: dry or wet. For dry-sanding, just apply the sandpaper to the piece.

This is not recommended unless you are wearing a particle mask. We recommend, for your health, to wet-sand. The water will absorb the tiny dust particles and prevent them from dispersing into the air and your lungs.

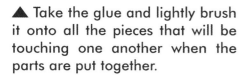

▲ For most modelling purposes, 400 and 600 grit wet-dry sandpaper are sufficient. 600 is finer, and should be used before priming.

■ *Wet Sanding*

▲ Take a piece of sandpaper and dip it in water. You will need to dip it again during sanding if it gets too dry.

▲ Lightly scuff the surface of the plastic until the normal plastic sheen no longer shows.

▲ After roughly a minute or two of sanding with wet sandpaper, the piece should be uniform and smooth.

■ SEAMLINE REMOVAL

Seam lines can diminish the look of a finished kit. There are many Gundam model kits that have been painted well, only to have their look ruined by unsightly seam lines. To some, these seam lines make the kit look too "toy-like".

There are two main methods used to remove seam lines. The first is transforming them into proper panel lines, complete with a panel line wash, by utilizing the Adze technique or by file. The second is to glue, putty and sand the seam line away (this will be covered later on in this book.)

There is a woodworking tool that also goes by the name 'adze'.

It dates back to the stone age, and could be used to perform the exact same technique as in this book in order to shape wood or soft materials.

■ Adze Technique

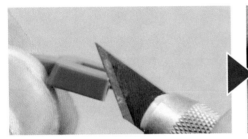

▲ Take a hobby knife and angle the blade as shown.

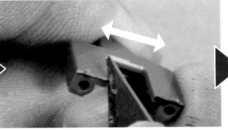

▲ Scrape the blade back and forth across the plastic. You may want to wear earplugs for this.

▲ Test-fit the pieces to ensure that it looks like a panel line.

Seam Line

Kit Piece 1 | Kit Piece 2

Kit Piece 1 | Design Knife

Converted Panel Line

Kit Piece 1 | Kit Piece 2

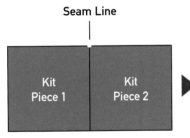

▲ To perform an adze with a file, make a consistent pen mark along the seam of the piece.

▲ File the pen away to leave a consistent groove. If there are any high or low spots, correct them.

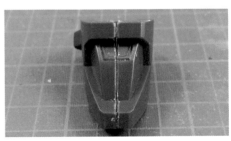

▲ Finally, sand and file the face of the pieces when together to ensure a smooth surface.

■ PANEL LINING

Applying panel lining gives the kit a more detailed look, compared to the look of ordinary, bare plastic.

Panel lining accentuates details that would normally be overlooked, such as ridge marks and panel lines.

There are two primary ways to apply this detail: by using special art pens or Gundam Markers, or using paint washes (the latter technique will be covered later on in this book.)

The most common panel line color used in Gundam modelling is black, but depending on the color of your kit, you can use a variety of colors such as brown, grey, or red.

We urge you to have fun with colors and see how they turn out.

▲ Gundam Markers and technical pens are readily available in a variety of colours.

 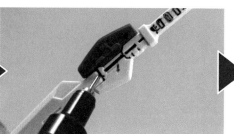 

▲ Take a fine marker and apply it to the channel in the piece. It can also be applied to accent corners.

▲ Draw a smooth line in the channel.

▲ Use a cotton swab, facial tissue, or even an eraser to wipe away the excess until only a thin line remains.

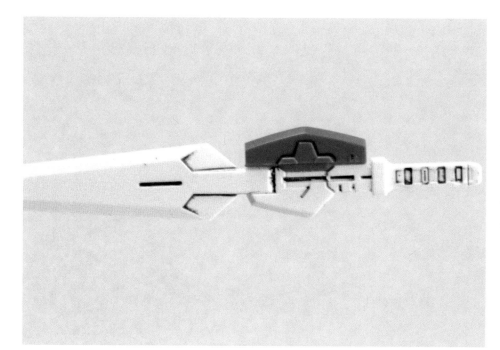

◀ Recently, many enamel-based, premade washes have become available in the market.

These products are easy to use, and are an alternative to markers.

The two techniques have various advantages and disadvantages, however we suggest beginners try pens before moving on to the slightly more advanced washes.

■ TOP COAT APPLICATION

The final step is to clear coat your model kit, also known as spraying on a top coat. This is where you spray a layer of clear paint to coat the kit.

The look you want your final kit to have will be partially determined by your top coat. Is the kit supposed to look like a gritty military suit? Then chances are you want a flat or matte coat, to dull the colours.

Is the kit supposed to be a brand new suit? Then try a gloss coat to make the colours more vibrant, or even a semi-gloss. Each type of top coat provides a different look to help you customize your builds even more!

■ Spraying Technique

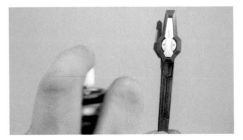

▲ Hold the can roughly 15- 30cm (6 - 12 inches) from the piece you wish to spray. Starting at one side of the piece, push the button down gently to start releasing the paint.

▲ Slowly move the can horizontally across the piece, releasing the nozzle once you have fully passed the piece. By starting to spray before and after spraying the piece, you can keep buildup on the nozzle from hitting the kit.

▲   Repeat until the piece is effectively coated. Patience is the key to spraying, as it is easy to accidentally overspray a very thick layer, which will force you to redo the piece. It's best to spray several, thinner coats instead.

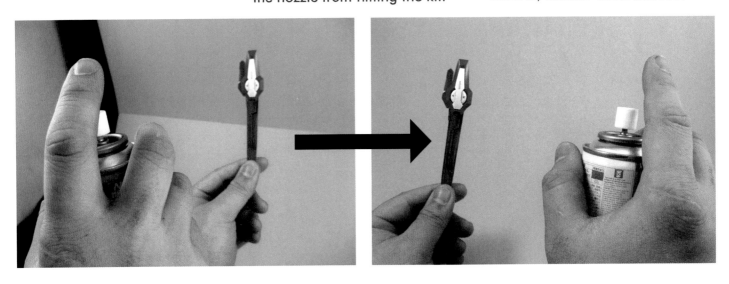

■ FINISHED KIT

PHANTOM
BLAZE ZAKU

× IAN KING

The 1/100 HG Blaze Zaku Phantom was released in March 2005 as part of the series *Gundam SEED Destiny*, which was much-contested in the west, but well-received in Japan.

Though not as popular as *Gundam Wing*, or even the original *Gundam SEED*, the model kits from this era were well-constructed and even showed significant development from the previous *Gundam SEED* models.

The Blaze Zaku Phantom was a re-imagining of the popular Zaku design that originated in the *Gundam* animated series (also referred to as *Gundam 0079* by fans.)

Although each series takes place in a different universe, the Zaku's basic design is often updated and re-used.

However, this is the only instance of a Zaku-like design retaining its original name.

For this kit, we'll be covering some basic techniques like planning the design, as well as beginning to work with paint, paint washes and some light weathering.

■ MODEL KIT PLANNING

Today, most modern plastic kits are prewashed in the factory. However, we recommend you wash your kits to remove any excess residue from the manufacturing process.

Wash your hands and refrain from handling food while building your kits.

Before you start working on any kit, it is a good idea to plan in advance. This will help you identify what steps you must take, decide what tools you need, and give you clear end goal. Advance planning can make a seemingly large, daunting task much more achievable. Plan your color scheme, what you want the kit to look like, and what you would like to achieve with the kit.

■ SANDING

Sandpaper is an abrasive used to remove material from surfaces. In the case of plastic, sanding is essential to prepare the plastic for painting, or to remove protruding nubs and seam lines.

  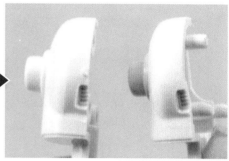

▲ Here we can see a protruding nub leftover from the cutting process.

▲ Sandpaper is used to remove the nubs, and then an emery board is used to polish the surface.

▲ This technique removes any sign of cutting by the nippers, even on unpainted plastic.

■ MISTAKES

No matter how easy to read the instructions are, mistakes will happen. In this case, you have to double-check and fix the problem. So if something seems off, double-check the step again.

 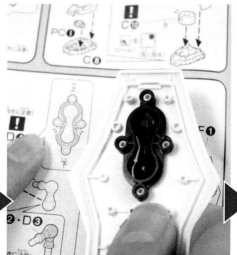 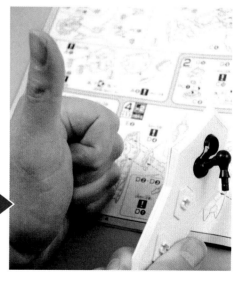

▲ As you can see, in our excitement we constructed this piece incorrectly, and now the joint piece is immovable.

▲ Looking back at the instructions, we can see that the piece was put in upside-down.

▲ Pay very close attention to the instructions, as some pieces must be oriented in a specific direction.

■ GAP & SEAM REMOVAL

Seam lines and gaps can easily ruin the appearance of a model kit. In order to improve the look of your kit, use glue and or putty to fill in the seam. Whether or not you use glue or putty is determined by the size of the gap of the seam line.

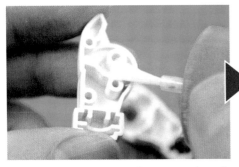

▲ To use cement glue, just brush it on the areas where the pieces of plastic join together.

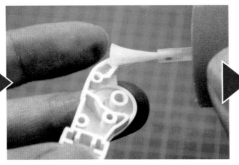

▲ Take care to coat all the sections that will be in contact with each other, to ensure a tight fight and to minimize gaps.

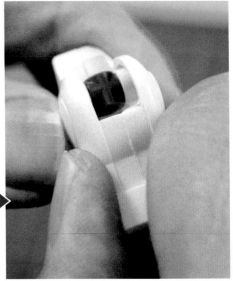

▲ Gently squeeze the parts together to let the cement ooze out a little bit. Once the cement is dry, wet-sand the seam line until it is smooth to the touch.

Tamiya putty can be made into a paste with hobby lacquer thinner. Mix a small amount of lacquer thinner and putty together to thin the putty. Then apply with a brush.

◀ If the seam line or gap is too large, use putty instead. Using a toothpick, liberally apply the putty in and around the gap.

◀ Once the putty has dried (can take 1 to 6 hours, depending on brand), wet-sand the puttied area.

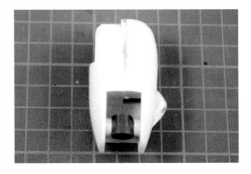

▲ If the gap in the plastic has not been properly filled, you will have to repeat the putty and sanding process until it is smooth.

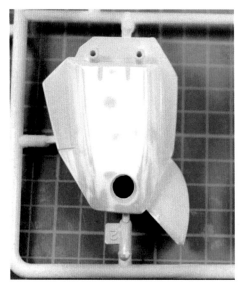

▲ Here, the parts have been primed and sanded to reveal the low spots and sink marks.

■ SINK MARKS

Sink marks are imperfections in the plastic which occur during the manufacturing process. As the plastic is ejected from the mold to cool, the thicker portions of the plastic cool slower than the thinner portions. This causes the thicker portions of the plastic to sag a little bit, creating irregularities on the surface of the plastic which are known as sink marks.

▲ Sink marks can be filled with with liquid putty and wet-sanded until smooth to the touch.

It's easy to see where sink marks are likely to occur by looking at the reverse side of a mold. Any areas where thick plastic suddenly turns thin are prime areas for sink marks.

You can also use a bright light to reflect off the surface of the part. Any low spots will be easy to see and fill before priming.

■ SANDING CURVED SURFACES

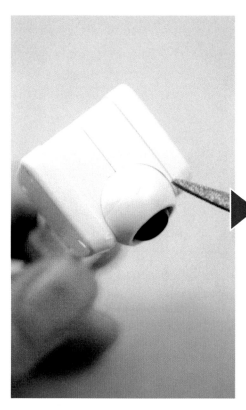

▲ Sometimes there are nubs and seams which appear on a curved surface. It is very easy to sand them flat if you are not careful.

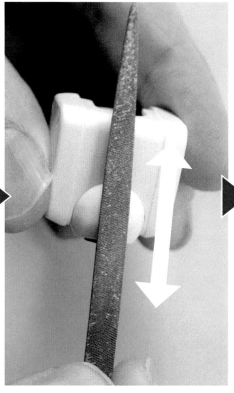

▲ Use a file to remove as much of the nub as possible, without removing it entirely. You will want a small buffer between the piece and the file.

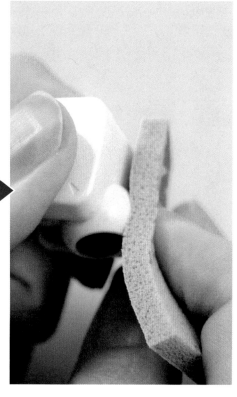

▲ Finally, use a sanding sponge to sand the surface until it is smooth to the touch.

■ MASKING & PAINTING

You may have noticed in the instruction manual that there are some pieces that should be multi-coloured, but the plastic is all one colour. This is where masking comes in. Masking is an essential skill when you start painting, if you are planning to achieve the colour separation that appears on the box.

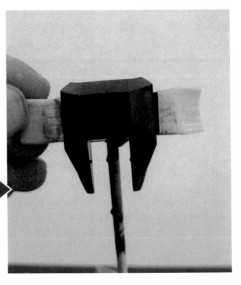

▲ Cut a length a masking tape to fit over the part you want to mask.

▲ Apply the tape so that it covers only the area you want to mask from the paint.

▲ After masking, secure the piece to a skewer with an alligator clip or sticky tack.

■ BASE COAT

It is very common for painters to cover a kit in a "base coat", which is achieved by painting all the parts in one solid colour. This can allow for a multitude of different techniques; in our case we will be spraying a lacquer silver to demonstrate paint chipping.

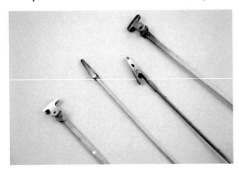

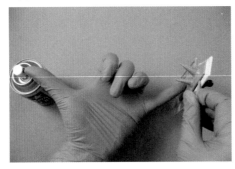

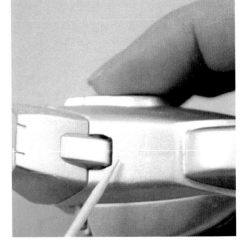

▲ Office clips, alligator clips and even sticky tack will hold parts while you paint them.

▲ As a rule of thumb, the distance for spraying should be about the length of your outstretched hand.

▲ Be sure to fill all the seam lines properly, or the else the paint will highlight every imperfection.

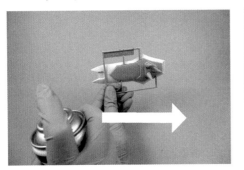

▲ Certain parts can be left on the sprue to make for easier spraying.

▲ In order to quickly paint as many pieces as possible, you can tape or tack runners to a cardboard box.

It is very important for the chipping method that the base coat be an oil-based paint (lacquer or enamel.) If you recall from our paint section, acrylic has the weakest bond while oil-based enamels and lacquers have the strongest. This makes oil-based paints the perfect candidate for the base coat, as they will resist the chipping we will be doing later on acrylic paints.

■ ACRYLIC TOP COAT

After the base coat has been applied, we will now paint the acrylic layer of paint over the base coat. This will be the colour of our model kit. The acrylic chosen to hand-brush here was Tamiya acrylic. When painting this layer, take care and paint in several light coats.

▲ Start by stirring the paint thoroughly. The consistency of the paint should be uniform.

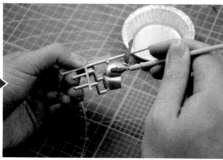

▲ Wet a brush with the thinner, and then dip it into the paint.

▲ When applying the first layer, it is very important to brush in one direction. Don't worry if it looks streak-y at first.

▲ Once the first layer has dried, brush on the second layer perpendicular to the way you brushed-on first layer.

▲ Using a small amount of acrylic retarder mixed in with the thinner can help prevent the paint from drying too quickly.

▲ When painting a large piece such as the shield, a wide brush is recommended to apply the paint with.

▲ As shown in the image, the first layer always has streaks and looks off. Don't worry, as you will be applying more coats of paint.

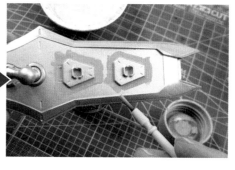

▲ For painting around raised areas, paint the edges around the area first, and then fill in the middle with paint in one direction.

■ SECONDARY MASKING

After the silver base coat has been applied, certain areas of some pieces need to remain silver in colour. To keep them the same colour, these areas are masked using low-tack painters' tape.

▲ Low-tack masking tape was used for this kit, as it won't harm the base coat of silver when peeled away from the piece.

▲ A toothpick is used to flatten the edges of the tape, allowing for easier cutting.

▲ Use the tip of the blade to cut away the excess tape, leaving only the exposed parts to be painted.

■ CHIPPING & WEATHERING

Now that the pieces have been coated in silver, masked, and the top acrylic layer has been applied, we begin chipping.

 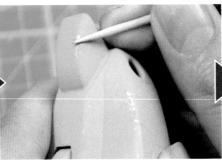 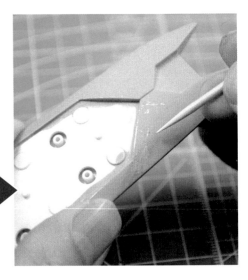

▲ Using a toothpick, the acrylic paint is scratched off, revealing the silver lacquer underneath.

▲ Chipping occurs mostly on the edges. Keep in mind that chips should be inconsistent.

▲Vary the pressure to provide a variety of chips.

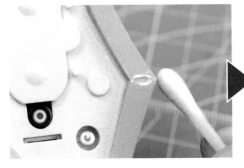  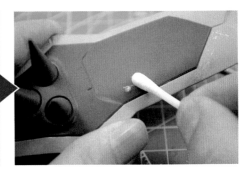

▲ Weathering can be done with alchohol-soaked cotton swabs to replicate fading of the top layer.

▲ Since the top is acrylic, keep in mind not much alcohol is needed.

▲ Try to make the chipping and fading 'tell a story', and not appear totally randomly.

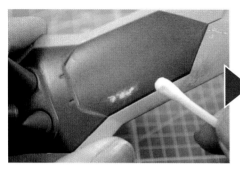

▲ Keep scale in mind, as the damage effects scale differently on a 1/144 kit than a 1/100 kit.

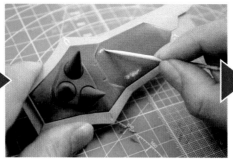

▲ Having many layers of paint an applying varied pressure while chipping give the model kit depth.

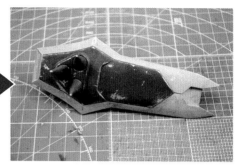

▲ The finished piece now shows the various types of weathering in different areas.

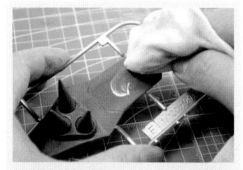

▲ White toothpaste can be used as an abrasive to lightly polish any rough surfaces in the paint.

▲ Once the piece is finished, spray a clear topcoat on to seal and protect the acrylics.

▲ A suitable distance for spraying topcoat is the same as paint: around 6-10 inches.

■ PAINT WASH

A wash is a mixture of highly thinned paint that is applied to model kits to bring out more details and provide depth. The wash flows into the panel lines and recesses, and is easily wiped off of the elevated areas of the kit. This wash is made with tempera paint from a dollar store, and was very affordable.

▲ Tempera paint is water soluble, which makes it easy to clean up.

▲ Mix a ratio of approximately 5% black paint and 95% water to make a very thin wash.

▲ Add a tiny drop of white to the wash in order to create more of a gray shade.

▲ Liberally brush the tempera wash onto the piece.

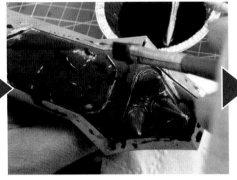

▲ Be sure to apply the wash along all panel lines and recesses in the kit.

▲ Allow the tempera wash to dry. Don't worry about any pooling or undesirable spots.

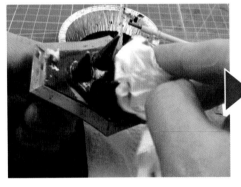

▲ Wet a paper towel with water, and wipe away the excess wash.

▲ The result is weathered piece with shading and pronounced panel lines.

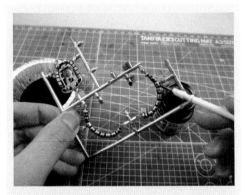

▲ Tamiya Smoke brushed over the silver pipes mimics grease buildup

■ UNMASKING

To finish up the earlier masking process, you can now spray a different colour over the pieces. Once the paint has cured, the tape is removed, revealing the two tones of colour that was planned for.

▲ The masked piece is sprayed with Tamiya German Gray.

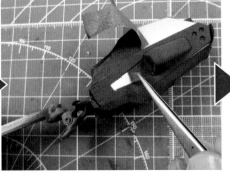

▲ Once the paint has cured, toothpicks can be used to lift the edges of the masking tape.

▲ Use tweezers to peel away the tape, showing the crisp colour separation on the piece.

■ **FINISHED KIT**

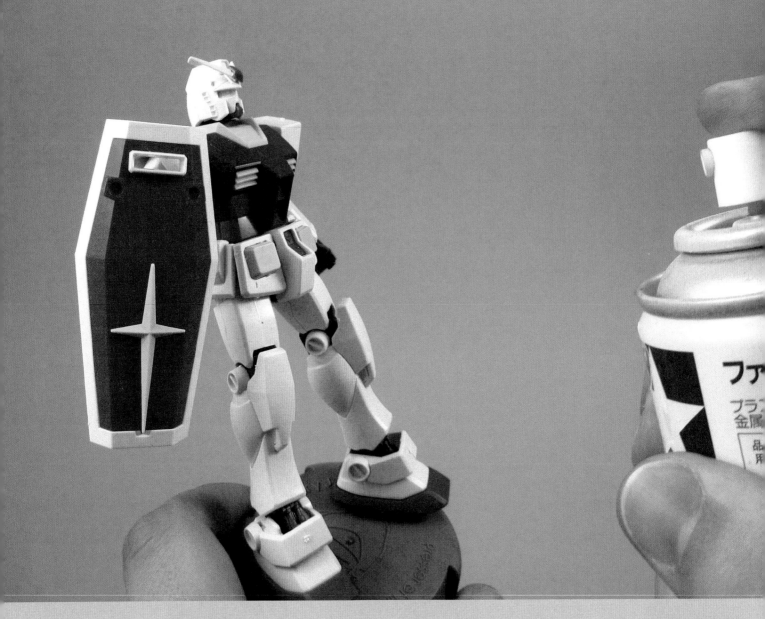

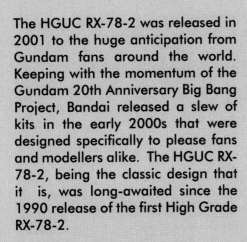

RX-78-2 GUNDAM

× NICK MCLEAN

The HGUC RX-78-2 was released in 2001 to the huge anticipation from Gundam fans around the world. Keeping with the momentum of the Gundam 20th Anniversary Big Bang Project, Bandai released a slew of kits in the early 2000s that were designed specifically to please fans and modellers alike. The HGUC RX-78-2, being the classic design that it is, was long-awaited since the 1990 release of the first High Grade RX-78-2.

It's easy to see the effort that Bandai engineers put into the HGUC Gundam. With easy colour separation and fantastic plastic quality, it was a wonderful new take on classic proportions, making it a sensation.

However, comparing the RX-78-2 to the modern High Grades of today, it is definitely showing its age, with its seam lines and noticeable lack of articulation. However, at the time of release, the articulation was

extremely good for a 1/144. The conscious efforts by designers to make the kit easy to build and easy to modify has helped it stand the test of time.

With this kit, we're going to show you more advanced techniques, such as simple colour separation, light weathering, removing panel lines and details, and adding battle damage.

■ ARTICULATION MODDING

When the HGUC line was first introduced, Bandai took great efforts to tailor the line to serious hobbyists, occasionally adding little 'Easter eggs' in the design to help modelers along.

With a little effort, it is possible to modify an old HGUC kit to have a much higher standard of articulation and colour separation. One of the key features of the HGUC Gundam is the easy-to-modify front skirt, which we will tackle first.

▲ Here we have the normal, unmodified front skirt. Pop the piece off the kit for modding.

▲ Normally, the front skirt is a single piece. The left and right sides cannot be moved independently.

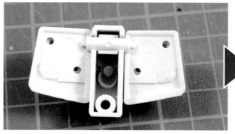

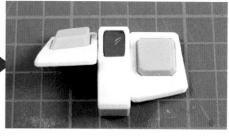

▲ Thankfully, the tabs fitting inside the waist piece are wide enough to support each side when separated.

▲ Carefully cut the front skirt in half down the middle. A sharp hobby knife or saw is best.

▲ When done properly, the skirt will be just as strong and now have one extra point of articulation.

▲ Before the mod, the limitations of the front skirt are obvious.

▲ When complete, the modified articulation will allow for more dynamic posing.

▲ Some kits are engineered to be easily painted with a few mods. Remove the tabs off the red torso piece, and glue it in after painting.

■ SUBTRACTIVE MODS

There are two basic types of sculpting techniques: adding materials and subtracting materials.

Similar to how a statue can be chiseled from a block of marble, we can use some basic tools and subtract materials from our Gundam kit to give it more depth. We are now going to focus on some subtractive mods on the RX-78-2.

▲ Due to consumer safety concerns, many kits with sharp points include little tabs on the end to prevent injury.

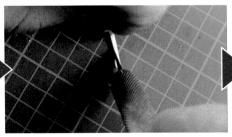

▲ To remove the tabs, simply make a straight cut with a sharp hobby knife, following the original line of the v-fin.

▲ Use a flat needle file to remove any excess material. A small bit of sanding with some 600 grit wet/dry sandpaper will finish the piece.

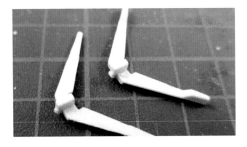

▲ As you can see from the above image, removing the tabs from the v-fin may seem like a minor detail, but it makes a difference to the aesthetic of the head.

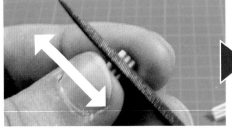

▲ Notches add detail and are simple to do! Run a square jewellers' file along the inside of the chest vents. Holding the file steady is paramount to this technique and can take practice.

▲ Take care not to file too much, or else you might file too deep into the plastic. Instead of filing the notch in one go, file a little at a time, and make sure you check if the notch is to your liking before you continue.

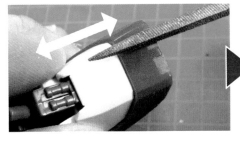

▲ You can make notches in other areas of the kit as well. The feet are a good example of this.

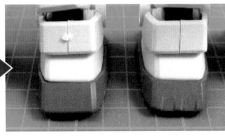

▲ Due to the small scale, absolute perfection isn't required. So don't worry too much, and remember this is for your own shelf.

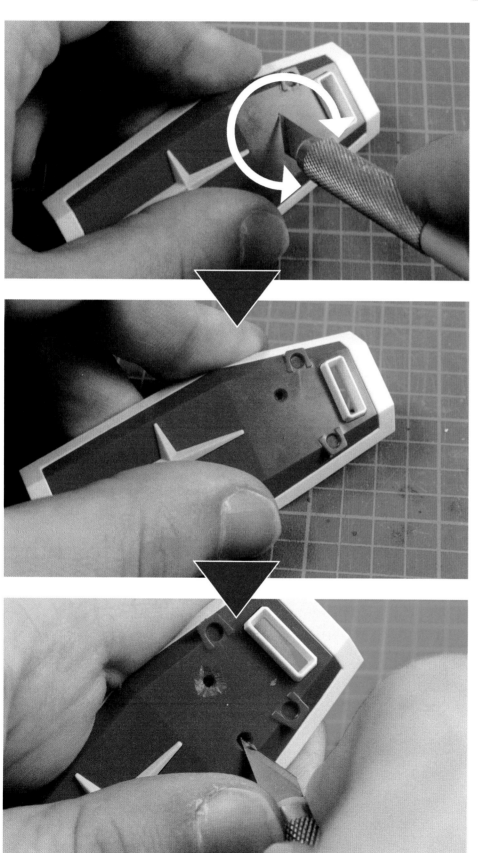

■ BULLET HOLES

◀ Unlike real life, there are many different ways to make bullet holes in Gunpla!

For this build, we're going to use a relatively simple and quick technique.

Using a sharp design knife, place the tip of the blade where you want the centre of the bullet hole to be. Spin the blade in a circle to drill out a hole. You can also use a pin vise to create the same effect.

◀ After turning your knife blade a few turns, you should have a cleanly-drilled hole in the piece.

To help you improve the placement of your battle damage, first ask yourself some easy questions. What kind of weapon was used, and how was the weapon used? A short controlled burst would cluster the impacts, whereas random fire would have several smaller impacts. Where would the suit most likely be damaged? At the back of the knee? Or could it have blocked the bullets with its shield?

◀ The last step is to use the knife, and perform wide angle cuts at the edges of the hole. Try to cut the edges randomly so that you give the hole a non-uniform look. This will add more depth to your bullet holes.

Practice is very important when learning subtractive modding techniques. We recommend keeping an old or spare kit for practicing on before you try techniques on your display piece.

■ PUTTYING YOUR KIT

Putty is very useful when painting a model kit. Soft putty, like Tamiya Basic Type (gray) is typically used for filling the seams between two adjoining parts after being cemented. After some filing and sanding, most seam lines should be barely visible. A good way to test is scratch with with your fingernail and see if it catches. If it does, you need to give it another go!

Modelers are often eager to add more detail to their kits. However, something that is not covered as often is the idea that removing certain details on your kit can give it more depth. A less-detailed kit can stand out just as much as a highly-detailed one.

▲ Here we can see a standard panel line; it is a surface detail molded into the kit.

▲ Squeeze out a little putty onto a toothpick.

▲ Using the toothpick, apply the putty to fill in the panel line thoroughly.

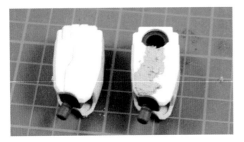

▲ The removed panel line on the leg won't show after filing or sanding away the excess. Sanding with 600 grit sandpaper will leave a smooth surface

▲ Putty can also be used to remove those pesky seam lines. Note: always cement the parts together before puttying.

Putty is also useful for removing sink marks. A sink mark is caused during the manufacturing process of the model kit, as the plastic is cooling down after being moulded. Thicker portions of the pieces tend to cool slower than thinner sections, causing some slight warping that is called a 'sink mark'.

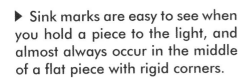

▶ Sink marks are easy to see when you hold a piece to the light, and almost always occur in the middle of a flat piece with rigid corners.

Here we have filled some sink marks with putty.

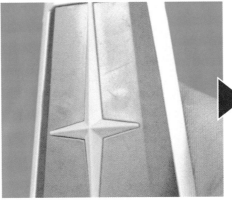

■ PRIMER PREPARATIONS

Getting ready for primer is a critical step in painting a model kit. After completing our mods, we cemented, filed and sanded the surface before applying putty to fill seams.

Next, the entire kit was sanded and inspected for imperfections in the surface. When you find a flaw or imperfection, fill it with putty and sand or file away to help remove the flaws.

There are two benefits to sanding a kit: first, it gives the surface of the kit micro-scratches, which give the primer something to hold onto. Secondly, it reveals low spots in the pieces.

◀ When preparing a kit to be primed, we suggest using 400 to 600 grit wet/dry sandpaper or above. You can also use lower grit sandpaper first to remove major details, and then re-sand the same piece with higher-grit sandpaper to smooth out the surface.

When sanding, you may notice that the sanded pieces look duller than the non-sanded pieces.

To put it simply, the kit isn't as reflective once you've sanded the surface, which makes it really easy to find the lowest points on the kit by looking for the shiny spots. Then all that's needed is some filing or sanding to buff out the imperfections.

Sanding can be a very tedious task and much patience is needed. We highly recommend putting in some DVDs or watching TV while you are sanding, to help pass the time.

■ SPRAY CAN ANATOMY

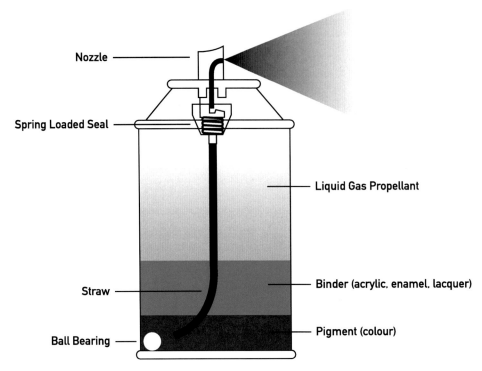

Nozzle

Spring Loaded Seal

Liquid Gas Propellant

Straw

Binder (acrylic, enamel, lacquer)

Ball Bearing

Pigment (colour)

In order to get the most out of our spray paints, it is important to learn how the spray paint can works. It's very easy to waste paint when we are beginning, or simply not being careful. So it's best to start with as much knowledge as possible.

Nozzle - This is usually a removable piece that dispenses the paint in a spray pattern. They come in a variety of different sizes and styles such as O shaped, fan spray, and splatter styles. Depending on the type of nozzle, it produces a different spray pattern. It is wise to test spray before painting your kit, and we suggest taking note of the spray pattern.

Most spray cans use a standard size tube for the nozzle to fit onto. This allows them to be interchangeable between brands and colours. Some art stores even carry specialized nozzles that can be used interchangeably with most spray cans. Make sure you keep

your nozzles clean, and save them when you recycle the can. We also recommended that you sort them by spray patterns.

Spring Loaded Seal - As you press down the nozzle head to release the can's contents, it compresses a spring which opens a seal, which allows the gas propellant to escape the can. As the gas escapes the can, it carries with it the paint pigments and thinner.

Straw -This is a long tube which goes down the length of the spray can. It is used to siphon the paint/gas mixture from the bottom of the can.

Liquid Gas Propellant - This is the driving force of the spray can. As the nozzle is pressed, it allows the gas to expand which pushes and pulls the paint mixture through the straw and out the nozzle.

Binder - Just like the binder we

described in the previous paint section, this contains the Acrylic polymer which binds the pigments together once the paint dries. The only difference is that there is also thinner mixed in with the spray can binder which determines if the paint you spray out is enamel, lacquer, or acrylic.

Pigment - This is the same things you can find in paint jars. They are small particles which give the paint it's particular colour. It is the heaviest part of the paint and always settles to the bottom of the can. Because of this, spray paint cans must always be shaken before use.

Ball Bearing - Also called the marble, this is used to mix the paint, binder, and propellant together by agitating the chemicals. Without the ball bearing, it would be difficult to mix the contents of the spray can thoroughly.

74

■ PRIMING

For this build we are going to apply the primer while the kit is completely assembled. This uses less primer, prevents the joints from sticking together (due to excess primer) and is far quicker.

The downside to this technique is that It might take a few coats to cover the entire kit. However, some kits may still have to be partially disassembled.

▲ Mount the kit onto a spray can cap using sticky tack, which makes it easier to spray from all angles. Be aware that sudden movements can cause the kit to fall.

▲ Be sure to hold the can upright and give it a good shake, primer particles are much heavier than paint and take longer to mix. It is also a good idea to warm up the can with warm water.

▲ When priming, the two most important things are the distance from the kit, and the speed of your arm. It is important to move your whole arm with the spray can and not just your hand.

We suggest to spray the hard to reach areas of the kit first. If you work your way out of corners you are at far less risk of over priming or painting your kit.

Don't begin spraying on the kit directly. Start spraying to the sides and the move the nozzle across the surface of the kit. This prevents possible buildup in the nozzle.

▲ When priming the kit, the speed of your arm dictates the amount of time the primer hits the kit, and the distance determines how concentrated the primer is.

The closer you are to the kit, the more primer hits it, but the faster you need to move your arm to keep the primer from excessively building up.

■ SIMULATED PAINT CHIPS

Fine-tipped brushes often come on a very thin brush, which can be a challenge to hold steady for many people. While lots of expensive brushes come with rubber grips, a good brush can be made better just by wrapping some tape around the handle. The thicker tape gives you more control while painting.

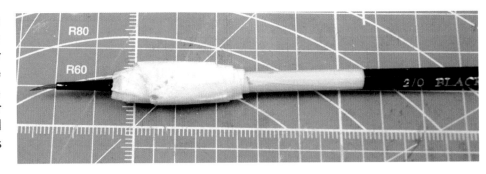

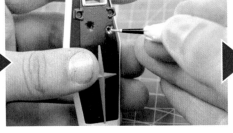

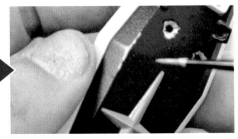

▲ Thoroughly mix some Tamiya aluminum paint. These Metallic paints are usually thicker than regular paint(due to the larger pigment), so spend a little more time mixing.

▲ Apply spots of the aluminum to certain areas and edges of the kit. The key to this placement is to ask yourself: " Where would paint chips naturally occur?"

▲ Applying the aluminum paint to the edges will enhance the kit as a whole, as paint tends to wear off the corners and edges first. A good question to ask yourself is: " Which parts will wear out first?".

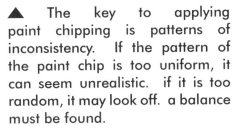

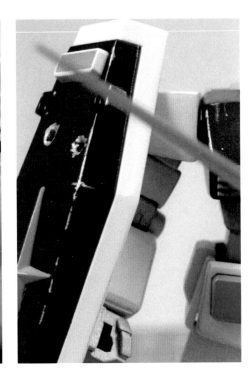

▲ The key to applying paint chipping is patterns of inconsistency. If the pattern of the paint chip is too uniform, it can seem unrealistic. if it is too random, it may look off. a balance must be found.

This is a simple technique and when used properly can really highlight certain areas of the kit.

■ STICKER & DECAL APPLICATION

 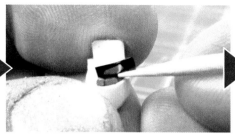 

▲ Peel away the sticker backing, exposing the glue of the sticker. Then use a toothpick or tweezers to grab the edge of the sticker and remove it.

▲ Carefully position the sticker and apply using a soft toothpick. Using a toothpick ensures a good placement of the sticker, and prevents fingers from removing the glue from the backing.

▲ When properly applied, some stickers can greatly enhance the appearance of a kit, and cut down on the time spent on the kit. However it is up to the modeler to decide what is best for each kit.

▲ Cut the decal from the sheet and submerge it in warm water. Water will loosen the decal bond between the backing paper and the decal itself.

▲ After 30-60 seconds of submerging the decal in warm water, the decal will release from the backing paper and become somewhat slippery.

▲ Use a toothpick (or your finger) to hold the decal in place and lift the backing paper from beneath the decal.

▶ Now that the decal is on the kit. You can reposition it with your toothpick. Take care not to use too much force as you may tear the decal.

Next, use a q-tip or paper towel to soak up the excess water from the surface of the kit and decal. Once both are dry, we suggest applying some decal softener.

Decal softener is used to "melt" the decals slightly so they conform to irregular shapes easily. However, be careful not to apply too much softener as it could cause your decal to dissolve.

■ **FINISHED KIT**

DEATHSCYTHE HELL CUSTOM

✕ DERICK SIU

The 1/100 HG Gundam Deathscythe Hell custom, also called H. Custom for the US release, was released in 1998 as a tie-in to the incredibly popular 3-part OVA Gundam Wing: Endless Waltz (released as a single movie in North America.)

While Endless Waltz was hugely popular in and of itself, the series that kicked it off, Gundam Wing, was responsible for the first big break for Gundam in the western world.

The series became so popular that its model kits, such as this one, could be found even in local toy stores.

Unfortunately, while the anime was incredibly popular, the model kits didn't quite fly off the shelves. This would be the only large-scale release of Gunpla in the west.

Despite its age, the Deathscythe Hell Custom was designed very well, and was even popular enough to receive the Master

Grade treatment in 2011.

With this kit, we're going to be exploring different uses of paint, namely, how to create a custom colour scheme, how to mask for painting, as well as some different ways to colour the panel lines.

We will also cover how to spot and fix defects in the plastic, and how to remove seam lines using melted plastic.

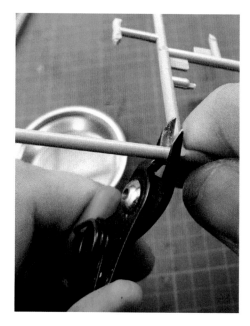

■ MODEL KIT PLANNING

Always, alway plan your kit in advance. In this case, we will be planning what colours to paint the Deathscythe Hell Custom. A good way to determine which parts should be painted certain colours is to use the line art provided in the instruction manual or by image searching. You can use colouring pencils/pens or Photo editing software to fill in different colours as you wish. Either way, this will help you gain a clear idea of what your model kit should look like once it is completed

For this kit, we're going break away from tradition by starting with the panel line colour. Usually, these lines are black, grey or brown. But we will use red instead, as it contrasts well against the black wings and grey limbs. We will add two tones of grey in certain areas, and to contrast the details further red stripes or veins."

■ CEMENTING FOR PAINT

  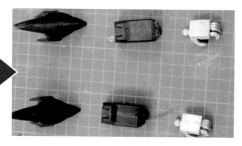

▲ Apply cement to both parts that will be glued together. "

▲ Once cement is applied, assemble the two pieces and squeeze them together tightly so that any excess cement comes out.

▲ Wait for the cement to dry, and sand away the excess cement on the surface.

■ SPOTTING IMPERFECTIONS

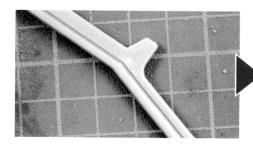  

▲ Some sink marks are formed when the sprue is ejected from the mold, while the plastic is hot. During cooling, the plastic shrinks rapidly in some areas.

▲ A good way to find sink marks is to sand the surface. Right away it will reveal any low spots and sink marks, which can then be sanded smooth.

▲ Some crevices may be hard to reach. By folding the sand paper so that the edge is round, you can get those hard-to-reach places.

■ FILLING SEAMS & SINK MARKS

We've already covered one way to correct seam lines and sink marks. In this section, we will revisit the putty technique, and introduce the melted plastic technique.

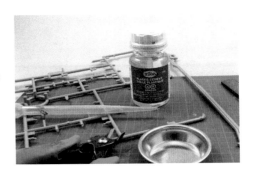

■ Using Melted Plastic

▲ Cut a sprue stick that is the same color as the seam line. This will ensure the melted plastic matches the original plastic colour.

▲ Using a bastard file, file shavings into a mixing cup.

▲ Once you have a good amount of sprue shavings, put a few drops of liquid cement and stir with a toothpick.

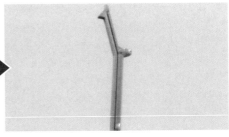

▲ The liquid cement will melt the plastic shavings, and you will be left with a gooey form of plastic, which can be used as putty.

▲ Take the mixture and apply it to the sink mark and/or seam line. Note: Do not use CA glue, as it is an adhesive and does not melt plastic.

▲ Once dry, sand it with 400-600 grit sand paper. This technique is particularly useful if you don't plan to paint, since the colours already match.

■ Using White Putty

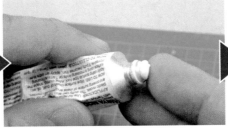

▲ Sand the piece lightly and check to see if the seam line is uneven.

▲ Apply a small amount of soft modelling putty. We used Tamiya White Putty on this kit.

▲ Once the putty dries, wet sand it first with a 400 grit, then follow up with a 600-800 grit to finish.

■ DEEPENING PANEL LINES

This technique is used to deepen the already-existing panel lines on a Gundam model kit, as some panel lines are shallow compared to others. As primer and paint are applied, a shallow panel line can become even shallower, to the point where it could disappear altogether. To prevent this, we deepen the panel lines around certain edges ensuring the channel exists for a panel line wash to flow into.

▲ Using the back of a hobby knife blade, place the tip at the starting point of the panel line.

▲ Firmly scrape towards the back of the hobby knife so that it scrapes the plastic.

▲ Be careful not to use too much pressure, as you can over-scribe the existing panel line.

■ SANDING SEAMLINES AFTER MASKING

On some models there are components with embedded parts, which makes it very hard to paint and remove the seam lines present. In the Exia build, turning a seam line into a panel line was the corrective method we used.

In some cases, you may wish to remove the seam line on the exterior panels. To do this, sand, surface, prime and paint the inner piece first. Then with masking tape, cover the piece and place the exterior pieces around the masked piece. With the DeathScythe Hell, we are using the red spike piece which fits into the exterior wings.

▲ Fill the hole and gaps with putty. Once dry, sand the piece smooth and prime it. Once the pieces are dry, spray paint them with your choice of colour

▲ Once the paint dries, use masking tape to seal up the entire piece. Make sure not to cover any attachment points

▲ Glue the exterior pieces together. Once the glue dries, apply putty to the seam line, and sand smooth. Now your kit is ready to be primed.

■ MISTAKES AFTER PRIMING

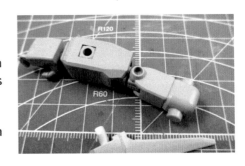

Once you have finished sanding and removing all the imperfections in the kit, you are ready for priming. For this example, Tamiya Primer was used to prime the Deathscythe Hell.

After the primer dries, you may notice more mistakes, such as seam lines you thought were sanded away or missed sink marks.

▲ Locate the mistake or neglected seam lines.

▲ Sand away the primer, refill the seam line with putty, and reprime.

▲ Inspect the primed piece to ensure the seam line is completely gone.

■ Spraying Mistakes

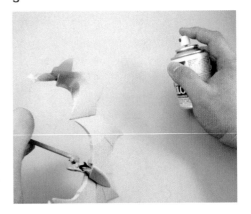

Two common mistakes when using a spray can are over-spraying and bubble pockets forming in your paint.

When the spray can has not been shaken or heated properly, the propellant within the can may condense within the paint. Normally when the propellant is expelled from the can, it will expand into the air. If the propellant gas is not mixed with the paint enough, there is a delay in this expansion. This delay causes the propellant to expand after it and the paint has contacted the kit. As a result bubble pockets form.

In the picture to your right, you can see pocket holes where the propellant has expanded after it has left the spray can.

To prevent such common mistakes from happening, make sure you:

1. Shake the can properly

2. Warm up the can of paint by placing it in warm (NOT BOILING) water.

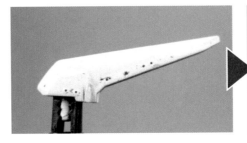 

▲ The first sign of areas where you may have oversprayed is when some of the lower layers of paint begin to show.

▲ The piece on the left shows what happens when you over-spray. This occurs when you move the nozzle of the spray can over a piece too slowly.

■ MASKING

To prepare masking tape, you'll need a cutting board, and ideally one with different types of guidelines. These lines will allow you to cut small and accurate strips of tape, which you can use t to create patterns or to mask off certain areas of a part, in order to spray the exposed piece of the plastic a different color.

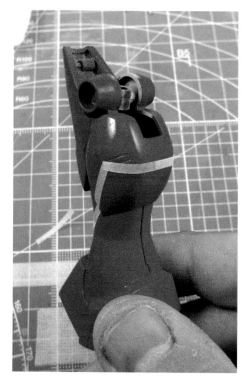

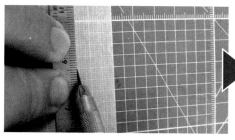 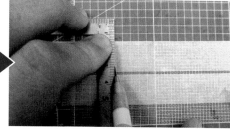

▲ Using a straight edge ruler, cut along the guidelines as best as possible. Make sure your knife follows the line, so that it does not stray and ruin the cut

▲ When cutting strips to proper size, make sure they are long enough to cover the pattern you want.

 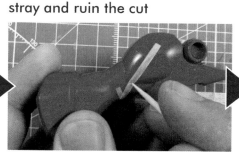 

▲ Lift the strips up carefully with the back of a blade, as to create a space for your tweezers to pick up.

▲ With your tweezers, gently lift up the strip, and place it on the piece to form a pattern.

▲ You can cut off any excess tape from your piece by gently cutting it with your knife, but be careful.

■ Masking Areas for Colour Separation

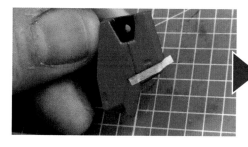 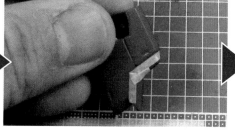 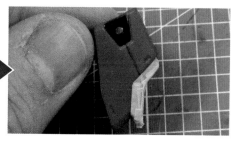

▲ When masking areas of the piece, smaller strips are better. These smaller strips can line up with different edges, especially irregular edges.

▲ Once the main edges have been masked, you can then use larger strips to mask any large areas of the piece.

▲ Once you place your masking tape, go over it with a toothpick to seal the tape over your piece. This ensures no paint will leak through.

■ Masking with Sticky Tack

Another way to mask patterns is to use sticky tack. This technique is commonly used to replicate the camouflage patterns you see on most military tanks and planes. The benefit to using sticky tack is that it creates a more feathered or softer border between the two colors. This is different than using masking tape, which creates a sharp and stark contrast on the border of the two different colours.

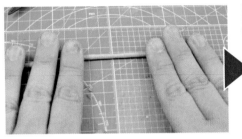

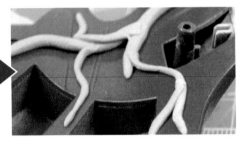

▲ Take a few pieces of sticky tack and roll them into several thin strips.

▲ Lay out the tack and ensure that it is sticking to the surface so paint can't seep under it.

▲ Check the areas where sticky tack contacts together, as the tack can be lifted up, which will allow paint to seep through.

■ SPRAYING OVER PAINTED PARTS

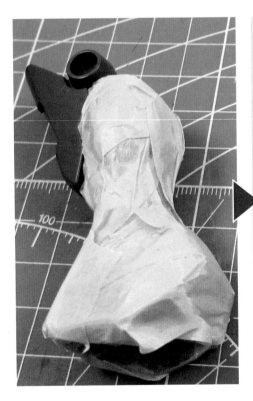

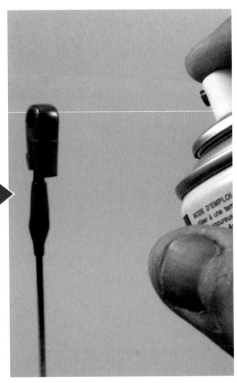

▲ Once you have your piece masked over, you can proceed to spray your next layer of paint.

▲ Mist your piece thoroughly. Wait 5-10 seconds for the sticky paint layer to develop.

▲ Proceed to spray your masked piece normally.

■ ENAMEL PANEL LINE WASH

The enamel panel line wash technique is commonly used to fill in the panel lines on model kits. Enamel paint is used because it does not damage the lacquer paint beneath it.

To do enamel panel line washes, you will need a brush, cotton swabs, a paper towel, and the enamel paint color of your choice (for this kit, we used red), lighter fluid, and two containers.

▲ Using a stir stick, make sure your enamel paint is properly mixed.

▲ Put a little drop of the enamel paint into a container.

▲ Pour some lighter fluid into both containers. Remember that the more lighter fluid you add, the lighter your panel line will be.

▲ With a brush, mix the paint and lighter fluid. The color should be blended so that the mixture is just under a milky consistency.

▲ Gently touch your brush to panel line and watch as the thinned color moves into the channel. This process is called "capillary action"

▲ Wait 5 minutes for the enamel paint to partially dry. Make sure not to wait more than 10 minutes as the paint can be partially cured.

▲ Dip a cotton swab into the container of lighter fluid.

▲ Wipe off the excess lighter fluid with a paper towel, so that it does not bleed onto the plastic

▲ Gently wipe off the excess enamel paint from the piece.

■ SHADING WITH GUNDAM MARKERS

One way to add more depth to a model kit, is by applying shading: AKA darkening the edges around a piece--usually this is done by using an airbrush, but there are other ways to do this as well.

In this example, we will explore how to get the shaded look by using Gundam Markers.

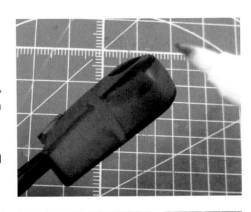

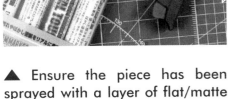

▲ Ensure the piece has been sprayed with a layer of flat/matte coat so the ink blends easily throughout the piece.

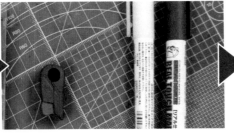

▲ Select the appropriate marker color. It should be a similar in color to the piece you want to shade, but slightly darker.

▲ Using the marker, line the edges with the darker color

▲ Using the Gundam "Real Touch" marker, blend the darker color with the surrounding piece. This will reduce the sharp contrast between the two colours.

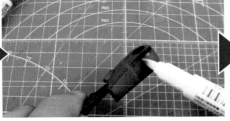

▲ The "Real Touch" marker is like a brush that uses a thinner specific to the ink in Gundam Markers. It can get clogged ink and will need to be regularly cleaned.

▲ To do this, just rub the marker onto a clean tissue paper. This will allow the extra ink to bleed into the tissue paper, thus cleaning the pen.

▶ Finally, you will see a result similar to preshading. With the markers, you can control your shading to make it sharper or lighter depending on your preference. In the image to the right, the piece on the left has been done with this method.

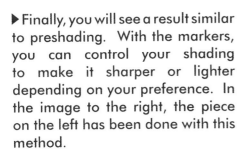
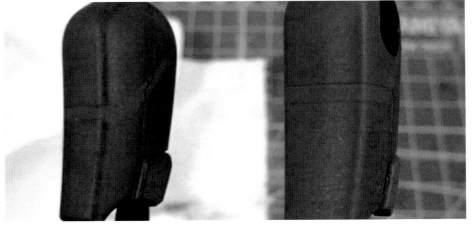

■ FINISHED KIT

■ IN CONCLUSION

As we come to the end of our journey together, we hope that this book has given you a glimpse into Mecha modeling -- and more importantly, we hope that the techniques covered in this book will help serve you as you continue your Mecha modelling journey.

Although we have covered many techniques throughout this book, keep in mind you do not need to use all of them.

Modeling is about expressing yourself through a medium, and so there are no 'rights' or 'wrongs'. Modeling is about what you would be proud to put on your own shelf.

There are many people who will putty every sink mark on every gundam they have, sharpen every part, and even do more advanced techniques--but there are just as many other people (if not more) who are happily satisfied by simply assembling the kit and perhaps adding a little panel lining.

Each model kit is only bound by your imagination, but that's not to say every model kit has to stretch your imagination to the extreme.

Sometimes you may find yourself appreciating a model design that you might want to keep exactly as it looked like in the show, and there's no wrong in that. However, if your interests are in modifying or painting the kit, eventually then we certainly hope the techniques in this book help.

One thing to keep in mind throughout your modelling career is that mistakes will happen, so it's best to be prepared, as it is a natural part of the learning process. Even though all four of us are experienced modellers, we have made and continue to make a lot of mistakes.

Mistakes expand your modelling skills. Sometimes mistakes are for the better, sometimes it causes you to cut your losses and move on to another kit. For that reason we highly suggest that you challenge yourself with no more than one or two new skills per build.

Gundam is a diverse multiverse made up of all kinds of different mecha suit designs. Each with it's own fan base. For example, some people are UC (Universal Century) die hards, while some others are Wing Gundam fans.

In other words, what appeals to you, may not appeal to someone else. Just like how some clean builds do not appeal to everyone.

This leads us to our final point: When entering this community be aware that not everyone will like everything you do, and learn how to separate legitimate criticism (IE: A puttied seam is still visible, or there's paint chipping, or scratches are visible) from personal preferences (IE: colour schemes, aesthetic modifications, sometimes even the universe the suit is from!)

Understand you can never, and really should never try to, please everyone with what you build. There will always be someone out there who doesn't like your style. We encourage you to change your focus to mastering the techniques that will allow you to build the best gundam in the style that most appeals to you.

Remember, the only one who has to 100% love your finished model is you, and always build for your own display case/shelf.

We hope you've all enjoyed this book and learned some useful tips from it, and we'd love to hear from you if you have any thoughts on how we can improve.

This book, like a model, is still a work in progress. so be sure to look out for future updates.

Best of luck, and enjoy your modelling journey!

Derick, Robert, Nick, Ian.

THANKS FOR READING!

Special Thanks to:

Becca Davidson, Dave Hovis, Gary Whintin, Chris Kultzow, Alan Britten, Simon Curry, Philip Nussbaum, Katsutoshi Katagiri, Francis Cane A Diaz, David Starshadow, Steven Lattenhauer II, Kendal Cormany, Jason Dooley, Thinh Haong Le, and the Scarlet Tinkerbell!

We thank you for your gracious support.

Made in the USA
Monee, IL
25 July 2020